# WRITERS GONE WILD

# Writers
# Gone Wild

The Feuds, Frolics,
and Follies of Literature's
Great Adventurers,
Drunkards, Lovers, Iconoclasts,
and Misanthropes

## BILL PESCHEL

A PERIGEE BOOK

A PERIGEE BOOK
Published by the Penguin Group
Penguin Group (USA) Inc.
375 Hudson Street, New York, New York 10014, USA
Penguin Group (Canada), 90 Eglinton Avenue East, Suite 700, Toronto, Ontario M4P 2Y3, Canada
(a division of Pearson Penguin Canada Inc.)
Penguin Books Ltd., 80 Strand, London WC2R 0RL, England
Penguin Group Ireland, 25 St. Stephen's Green, Dublin 2, Ireland (a division of Penguin Books Ltd.)
Penguin Group (Australia), 250 Camberwell Road, Camberwell, Victoria 3124, Australia
(a division of Pearson Australia Group Pty. Ltd.)
Penguin Books India Pvt. Ltd., 11 Community Centre, Panchsheel Park, New Delhi—110 017, India
Penguin Group (NZ), 67 Apollo Drive, Rosedale, North Shore 0632, New Zealand
(a division of Pearson New Zealand Ltd.)
Penguin Books (South Africa) (Pty.) Ltd., 24 Sturdee Avenue, Rosebank, Johannesburg 2196,
South Africa
Penguin Books Ltd., Registered Offices: 80 Strand, London WC2R 0RL, England

While the author has made every effort to provide accurate telephone numbers and Internet addresses
at the time of publication, neither the publisher nor the author assumes any responsibility for errors
or for changes that occur after publication. Further, the publisher does not have any control over and
does not assume any responsibility for author or third-party websites or their content.

Copyright © 2010 by Bill Peschel
Text design by Kristin del Rosario

First edition: November 2010

Library of Congress Cataloging-in-Publication Data

Peschel, Bill.
  Writers gone wild : the feuds, frolics, and follies of literature's great adventurers, drunkards,
lovers, iconoclasts, and misanthropes / Bill Peschel.— 1st ed.
    p.   cm.
  Includes bibliographical references and index.
  ISBN 978-0-399-53618-2
  1. Authors—Miscellanea.   2. Literary curiosa.   I. Title.
  PN165.P47 2010
  809—dc22 [B]                         2010023601

PRINTED IN THE UNITED STATES OF AMERICA

10  9  8  7  6  5  4  3  2  1

Most Perigee books are available at special quantity discounts for bulk purchases for sales promotions,
premiums, fund-raising, or educational use. Special books, or book excerpts, can also be created to
fit specific needs. For details, write: Special Markets, Penguin Group (USA) Inc., 375 Hudson Street,
New York, New York 10014.

*To Teresa*

# Contents

PART THREE: Everything Else                          149

# Introduction

George Bernard Shaw inspired this book. Particularly his condoms.

On July 18, 1885, the poor, unknown Irishman, scraping by in London on journalism and in lust with the older Jenny Patterson, bought a packet of "French letters." After examining them thoroughly, he noted in his diary both the price—5 shillings—and that they "extraordinarily revolted me."

When I read the story 109 years later in Michael Holroyd's excellent four-volume biography, something clicked in my head. My immature imagination had conceived of writers as special, sparkly people. They still are, to me. But they're also like me: fallible, fumbling, and sometimes foolish. Shaw was no longer just the genius playwright who knew what was good for us, including vegetarianism, simplified spelling, and communism. He became human, carefully counting his pence and fretting about sex, what he would later call in his diary the "novel experience" with Jenny that marked his twenty-ninth birthday.

Shaw's story was so fascinating that I noted the affair, with its near

*Fatal Attraction*–like conclusion, and amused myself with the idea of creating a book of days, with "holidays" marking silly and serious milestones in writers' lives. Over the years, I added to this collection: from biographies sent to me for review and books scarfed up at library sales.

Then the Internet came along. I discovered English newspapers writing about Dylan Thomas dodging machine-gun bullets, Mario Vargas Llosa decking Gabriel García Márquez, and Somerset Maugham slamming Hugh Walpole. On a personal website, someone posted a long essay about the day Henry David Thoreau burned down a forest. Both *The Writer's Almanac* with Garrison Keillor and Steve King's "Today in Literature" provided inspiration. Wikipedia supplied leads on the reaction to Alfred Jarry's *Ubu Roi* and Johann Goethe's *Sorrows of Young Werther*. Novelist Jonathan Ames's too-brief Literary Dick blog examined Henry James's mysterious injury and Mary McCarthy's interest in penises.

When my book-of-days idea morphed into *Writers Gone Wild*, Google Books supplied contemporary accounts of John Milton's exhumation, Jacqueline Susann's anger at President Kennedy getting himself assassinated, Dostoyevsky's near-execution, O. Henry's stint in prison, and Robert Burns's shagging. By this time, my worry wasn't so much about finding enough great stories but deciding which ones to tell.

Some will call this book a collection of gossip, to which I will stand at the bar and plead guilty. In mitigation, it is through gossip that we experience life's rich variety, and it gives us the opportunity to understand and empathize with the struggles these artists endured and lets us draw connections between their lives and their works. Great books do not arise in a vacuum, but from the humus of daily living.

Plus, they're great fun to read.

And if you meet the spirit of George Bernard Shaw before I do, tell him I'm sorry. Sort of.

BILL PESCHEL
HERSHEY, PENNSYLVANIA

## · PART ONE ·

# On the Job

·1·

# Dramatic Debuts

Iconoclastic, shocking, or just plain
weird, these works inspired tsunamis
of outrage.

## Johann Goethe: Threat or Menace? (1774)

The next time you're told that rock music, graphic novels, and violent video games are corrupting our youth, remember that German
novelist Johann Wolfgang von Goethe got there first. At age twenty-
three, his tale of a doomed youth, *The Sorrows of Young Werther*,
thrilled readers and outraged moralists.

Like a Teutonic Holden Caulfield, the sensitive romantic Werther
is disgusted with society's hollow values. Passionately in love with
Lotte, he prefers to die rather than see her marry the dull, plod-
ding Albert and, in an ironic twist, shoots himself using her fiancé's
pistols.

Goethe found inspiration for his story close at hand. As a newly
minted lawyer in Wetzlar, he was befriended by Karl Jerusalem, who
introduced him at a ball to Johann Kestner and his fiancée, Charlotte. Goethe fell deeply in love with the nineteen-year-old girl, but
she preferred her stolid Johann. Distraught, Goethe fled Wetzlar but
remained in touch with the couple and even attended their wedding.

Goethe wasn't the only man unhappily in love. When a married woman rejected Jerusalem, he borrowed two pistols from Kestner and shot himself. Goethe combined his misery with Jerusalem's tragedy and wrote his debut novel in only four weeks.

*The Sorrows of Young Werther* became *the* book to read in 1774. The official edition was translated into several languages, and pirated editions flooded the market. Writers jumped on the bandwagon with their *Werther*-like stories. Manufacturers cranked out fan memorabilia such as bread boxes decorated with scenes from the novel and porcelain statues of Werther and Lotte. Young men copied Werther's signature outfit of a blue frock coat with tin buttons, leather waistcoat, brown boots, and a round felt hat. Poor Jerusalem's grave became the site of candlelit ceremonies.

But some countries banned the book when several men, and at least one woman, followed Werther's lead and committed suicide, forcing the publisher to add to later editions a warning from Werther to "be a man and do not follow after me."

Everyone was happy with *Werther*'s success, it seems, except the Kestners. "The real Lotte would . . . be grieved if she were like the Lotte you have there painted," Herr Kestner wrote Goethe. As for Albert, he moaned, "Need you have made him such a blockhead?"

Goethe tried to make amends, but he couldn't help crowing a little. Tell Charlotte, he said, "to know that your name is uttered by a thousand hallowed lips with reverence, is surely an equivalent for anxieties which would scarcely . . . vex a person long in common life, where one is at the mercy of every tattler."

Perhaps. It could also be that—to a man rejected in love—success is the best revenge.

## Baudelaire's Evil Flowers (1857)

When it comes to disaffected, dissipated poets, Charles Baudelaire stands alone. He drank heavily and indulged in laudanum. He caroused with prostitutes, especially Jeanne Duval, with whom he was madly in love but who didn't care for him except when he had money. He spent his francs foolishly, running through an inheritance within two years and borrowing heavily from anyone unwise enough to lend him money. Considering his indulgences, it's a wonder he reached forty-six before dying.

Baudelaire's weaknesses were matched by his groundbreaking poetry and his ability to spot talent. As a critic, he championed the works of Edouard Manet, Richard Wagner, and Eugène Delacroix. His translations of Edgar Allan Poe helped boost Poe's reputation in America.

Baudelaire's rampage through the wild side of life found its ultimate expression in his notorious poetry collection *Fleurs du Mal*. The *Flowers of Evil* covered all the targets, attacking society, religion, and hypocrisy and praising death, decadence, and the erotic. As Baudelaire put it: "I put my entire soul, my entire heart, my entire religion, my entire hatred into that horrible book."

For its distillation of concentrated evil and sex, *Fleurs du Mal* rivals a Marilyn Manson album. The poet in "The Taste for Nothingness" sought oblivion from his dark heart. "Lesbos" praised that legendary Greek island with images of maidens fondling themselves before mirrors. "The Vampire's Metamorphoses" combined both sex and despair with a touch of Stephen King; describing an erotic encounter in which the sated narrator turns to his lover and sees a faceless, putrescent monster.

Unfortunately for Baudelaire, the French authorities caught wind of *Fleurs du Mal*, and ordered the print run to be seized and the author charged. Baudelaire was found guilty of insulting public decency, fined 300 francs, and ordered to suppress six of the poems. It would take more than ninety years for the French government to reverse its verdict and lift the ban.

---

French newspapers went into conniptions over *Fleurs du Mal*, especially *Le Figaro*: "The odious is cheek by jowl with the ignoble—and the repulsive joins the disgusting. You have never seen so many bosoms being bitten, chewed even, in so few pages; never has there been such a procession of demons, fetuses, devils, cats, and vermin."

---

## That "Cheap and Pernicious" Huck Finn (1885)

Mark Twain didn't think much of the book, a crude prank nearly sank it before publication, and even today, it's been banned for racism, crudity, and obscenity. Yet, like the Mississippi River it's set on, *The Adventures of Huckleberry Finn* just keeps rolling along.

After his success with *The Adventures of Tom Sawyer*, Twain intended to write a money-spinning sequel that would again nostalgically evoke his childhood. But Huck wouldn't play nice, and the novel kept sailing into darker waters. After eight years of on-and-off writing, Twain realized that Huck's flight from his abusive father down the river with the slave Jim would let him say things about race, freedom, greed, and vice.

But Huck wasn't done with giving Twain trouble. To make more money, Twain had formed a company to publish the novel by subscription. As the novel was being printed, agents equipped with sample copies fanned out across the country. One of them discovered that a devilish engraver had altered an illustration of Uncle Silas to make it look as though he was exposing himself to Huck.

Panic ensued. Frantic messages were sent to printers in the United States, Canada, and England to stop the presses, and the few shipped copies were recalled and destroyed. The offending page was ripped from every agent's copy. The damage control was so successful that no example of the vandalized illustration survives, but the book missed the lucrative Christmas season and news of the gaff tainted its reputation.

Critics greeted *Huckleberry Finn* with mixed reviews. The *New York World* called it "cheap and pernicious stuff," and *Life* magazine drolly suggested that Huck's faking his murder by killing a pig with an ax "can be repeated by any smart boy for the amusement of his fond parents."

But Twain cheered up when the public library in Concord, Massachusetts, banned the book. By calling it "trash and suitable only for the slums," he crowed, "that will sell 25,000 copies for us sure."

## Alfred Jarry and the *Ubu Roi* Riots (1896)

Although he was only twenty-three, Alfred Jarry was already notorious on Paris's artistic scene, both for his fondness for absinthe—a semi-poisonous liquor that he called the "green goddess"—and for his iconoclastic plays. His first play, *Caesar Antichrist*, for example, intimated that Jesus was resurrected after his crucifixion to become an agent of the Roman Empire.

But taking on religion was small beer compared to *Ubu Roi*, which attacked everything within reach, including royalty, militarism, and humanity. The drama plays off *Macbeth*, as Pa Ubu and Ma Ubu scheme to kill King Wenceslas and take over Poland. But in place of the haunted title character of Shakespeare's tragedy, Jarry portrayed Pa Ubu as gross, obscene, grasping, vindictive, gluttonous, murderous, cowardly, and—worst of all—victorious. Small wonder that the Parisian playgoers, split between fans of the avant-garde and the traditionalists, prepared to do battle on opening night.

The trouble started with Pa Ubu's first word—*merdre*—the Jarryesque variation on the French word for excrement that has been translated into English as "shee-yit," "shite," or "shitsky."

For fifteen minutes, the play stopped dead as the audience hooted, clapped, and cheered. Some walked out in anger, and others threw punches. It seemed as if the actors became the audience and watched the drama unfold in the seats.

The crowd quieted down only when the houselights were turned up, and Pa Ubu danced a jig before pretending to pass out. Then Pa Ubu said *merdre* a second time, and all hell broke loose again.

So it went for the rest of the evening, and the next night as well. The actors had to mime their dialogue over the catcalls to finish the play. After the second night, the French authorities had had enough and banned *Ubu Roi*.

## Mencken Loses His Religion (1920)

At a party in New York City, critics H. L. Mencken and George Jean Nathan were introduced to a writer who thought he was God's gift to literature. The man was tall and skinny, his hair the color of paprika, and he drunkenly snaked his arms around their necks and lectured them in his broad German-Minnesota accent that he was the best writer in this "gottdamn" country. He told "Georgie" and "Hank" that his first book would be published soon, that "it's the goods," and concluding, "You've got a treat coming, Georgie and Hank, and don't you boys make no mistake about *that*!"

"Of all the idiots I've ever laid eyes on," Mencken said after the drunk left them, "that fellow is the worst."

But when he read Sinclair Lewis's *Main Street*, Mencken wrote to Nathan:

*Dear George:*

*Grab hold of the bar-rail, steady yourself, and prepare yourself for a terrible shock! I've just read the book of that Lump we met at Schmidt's and, by God, he has done the job! It's a genuinely excellent piece of work. Get it as soon as you can and take a look. I begin to believe that perhaps there isn't a God after all. There is no justice in the world.*

*Yours in Xt.,*
*M[encken]*

---

When he was an unknown, Sinclair Lewis made a few dollars selling story plots to Jack London, who admitted that he couldn't construct plots "but I can everlastingly elaborate." London continued to help Lewis even after he caught him cribbing some of his ideas from O. Henry.

---

## Radclyffe Hall Empties the Well (1928)

Virginia Woolf called the novel so dull that "one simply can't keep one's eye on the page." The author's lawyer labeled it an "over-sentimental bit of Victorian romanticism." But judges in two countries deemed it obscene, and a newspaper editor wrote he'd "rather give a healthy boy or girl a phial of prussic acid than this novel."

The poison in question was *The Well of Loneliness* by Radclyffe Hall, a lesbian who called herself "John," affected mannish dress, and favored green cigars when she wasn't chain-smoking cigarettes.

*The Well of Loneliness* contained no sex scenes or obscene words, but Hall's third novel was still hot stuff. Up until then, lesbian writers had avoided controversy by switching the sex of their characters or coding their passions with vague descriptions and euphemisms. The story of Stephen Gordon's life as a "female invert" minces no words as she struggles to understand herself, find a lover, and beg God to "give us also the right to our existence!"

The publisher, Jonathan Cape, tried not to draw attention to the book. It was printed in a plain black binding, and an introduction was added by the respected sex theorist Havelock Ellis, whose interest in lesbians became personal after his wife ran off with one.

It almost worked. The reviews in the respectable newspapers were positive. Then the down-market *Sunday Express* discovered it. Editor James Douglas blasted *Well* as "evidence of a pestilence afoot which is devastating young souls" and demanded that its publisher withdraw the book or the government suppress it.

Cape halted the printing press after Britain's home secretary ruled the book obscene, but shipped the plates to Paris, where *Well* became an underground bestseller. Hall watched with amusement as European publishers outbid each other for the translation rights.

"Oh well, as long as we get the dollars!!!" she wrote.

## *Howl*'s Moving Telegram (1955)

At a reading on Fillmore Street in San Francisco, Allen Ginsberg's *Howl* electrified American poetry.

For Ginsberg, the performance was the culmination of months of personal upheaval. At twenty-nine, the Columbia University graduate had lost his way. He couldn't get his poems published, he was conflicted over his homosexuality, and he was feeling guilty over authorizing his mother's lobotomy. When Neal Cassady's wife threw him out of her house after catching him giving her husband oral sex, Ginsberg was forced to move.

His luck changed in San Francisco, with its thriving arts scene and tolerance for homosexuals. Ginsberg began a new poem, starting with "I saw the best mind angel-headed hipster damned" from a journal entry about an institutionalized friend. He threw in references to his mother's lobotomy and his homosexuality and his fears about the Cold War and the future of America. He added shout-outs to his friends from Columbia such as Jack Kerouac and William S. Burroughs. One night, high on peyote and wandering the streets, he encountered the Sir Francis Drake Hotel and dubbed it Moloch, after the Canaanite fire god to whom children were sacrificed. The vision seemed to him the perfect metaphor for America.

Ginsberg had not intended to publish *Howl*. It was a private poem, so he felt free to experiment and exorcise some demons. But when he was asked to organize a poetry reading at the Six Gallery, he decided to perform it there.

Thanks to Ginsberg's marketing skills, a couple hundred people showed up for the reading at the gallery, which had been converted from an auto body shop. Kerouac sat near the platform, passing around jugs of cheap burgundy. Several local poets read, but Ginsberg's incendiary performance brought down the house. As he rolled through the lines, the audience responded, and Kerouac egged him on by shouting "Go! Go! Go!" As the audience cheered, Allen left the stage transformed and in tears.

The next day, borrowing Ralph Waldo Emerson's response to Walt Whitman regarding *Leaves of Grass*, publisher Lawrence Ferlinghetti sent Allen a telegram that married art and commerce. "I greet you at the beginning of a great career," he wrote. "When do I get the manuscript?"

## Capote's Answered Prayer (1975)

After his success with *In Cold Blood*, Truman Capote wanted his next novel, *Answered Prayers*, to be his masterpiece, the novel that would make him the American Proust. Instead, he was labeled an American Judas.

For years, Capote had wormed his way into New York's high society and its blend of old wealth and new power, and as he dazzled them with his wit at their dinner parties and on their yachts, he quietly watched and noted their affairs and scandals.

Two stories in particular caught his attention. In 1955, the heir to the Hanover banking fortune, Bill Woodward, was shot to death in the dark by his wife, Ann, who had mistaken him for a burglar. Although the shooting was ruled accidental, his mother (who had never liked Ann) thought he had been murdered.

Truman also heard a story that Bill Paley, the powerful head of CBS and the husband of his longtime gal pal, Babe, was nearly caught with another woman.

He incorporated these stories—and others drawn from his memories, diaries, and letters—and wrote several chapters. When he sold four of them to *Esquire* magazine, his friends warned Capote that his society friends would see themselves in it. "Nah, they're too dumb," he replied airily. "They won't know who they are."

Publication of the "La Côte Basque" excerpt caused an earthquake among New York's high and mighty that, Capote wrote, "ranged from the insane to the homicidal." Ann Woodward fatally overdosed on Seconal. Slim Keith, whom Truman warned was in it but not as the central character, felt betrayed. Gloria Vanderbilt threatened to spit on him. Babe, by then dying of cancer, ostracized Truman. By the time the last excerpt appeared, New York society had banished Capote.

While Capote talked about the book for the rest of his life, friends such as Andy Warhol theorized that he was so traumatized by the uproar that he couldn't finish it. Despite the rumors of notebooks containing the finished manuscript, nothing was found after his death.

*Prayers* haunted Capote for the rest of his life. "I dream about it and my dream is as real as stubbing your toe," he said. "Part of

# The Trials of James Joyce
## (1914–1939)

The literary writer with probably the biggest drama-to-publication ratio would have to be James Joyce. Three out of his four major works provoked condemnation, bans, and outright head-scratching.

- Publication of his *Dubliners* (1914) was delayed for eight years owing to its stark portrait of the Irish and its use of obscene words—such as *bloody*. One printer refused to set certain words in type, and Joyce refused to rewrite them. Despite the controversy, the book's reception was met with indifference, and Joyce bought most of the books himself.
- *Ulysses* (1922) caused trouble in 1919 when issues of "The Little Review" containing "obscene" excerpts were seized and burned and its editors fined. The novel was banned in the United States until 1933.
- Published in 1939, *Finnegans Wake*'s obscure text provoked objections from nearly everyone in Joyce's circle and supporters such as Ezra Pound, H. G. Wells, and Joyce's patron, Harriet Weaver. But Joyce's contention that "I can justify every line of my book" has been borne out by scholars.

my brain says, 'The book's so beautiful, so well constructed—there's never been such a beautiful book.' Then a second part of my brain says, 'Nobody can write that well.'"

---

While Capote's reputation was hurt by *Answered Prayers*, he thought *In Cold Blood* nearly killed him. To research the Clutter murders, he befriended their killers and watched their execution before finishing the book. The book, he said, "scraped me right down to the marrow of my bones."

# ·2·

# Public Embarrassments

*When it's hard to apologize around
that foot in your mouth.*

## Sedley's Obscene Frolic (1663)

Sir Charles Sedley was a noted wit, poet, playwright, and friend of King Charles II. He was also a notorious carouser, and one of his escapades landed him in court and into the diary of Samuel Pepys.

One day, Sedley went with two nobles to Oxford Kates, a popular cook's house on Bow Street, Covent Garden, and proceeded to get stinking drunk.

Afterward, Pepys wrote, Sedley appeared on the second-floor balcony and before a thousand Londoners "showed his nakedness . . . acting all the postures of lust and buggery that could be imagined, and abusing of scripture and . . . preaching a Mountebanke sermon from that pulpit, saying that there he hath to sell such a pouder as should make all the cunts in town run after him."

Sedley then raised the bar for performance art from obscenity to blasphemy by imitating the moment in Communion when the priest dips the host into wine, only with a slight difference: "He took a glass of wine and washed his prick in it and then drank it off; and then took another and drank the King's health."

To round out the performance, Sedley and his friends pulled down their pants and, as another gossip noted, "excrementiz'd in the street."

Their audience responded by rioting, smashing the windows with rocks, and trying to break inside. Sedley and his companions barely escaped with their lives.

At his trial for blasphemy, the judge tried to shame Sedley by asking if he had read *The Complete Gentleman*, a popular guidebook. Aristocratic to the bone, Sedley coolly replied that he had certainly read more books than the judge.

As a result, Sedley was fined £500, jailed for a week, and forced to post a bond to ensure good behavior for the next three years. It may seem like a stiff penalty, but remember that, as late as 1648, the usual punishment for blasphemous acts involved disemboweling the miscreant. By that standard, Sedley got off light.

## Voltaire Gets Beaten (1717)

When he wasn't trying to become an aristocrat, Voltaire couldn't help making fun of them, which at times found him on the wrong end of someone's fist.

In 1715, when Voltaire was just twenty-one, he was exiled from Paris for writing poems satirizing regent Philippe d'Orléans for bedding the duchesse de Berry, who also happened to be his daughter.

Allowed to return a few months later, Voltaire wrote an anonymous poem again satirizing the incestuous relationship. But then he got drunk and bragged about it to an informer named Beauregard.

That was bad enough, but he also complained to the spy, "Do you know what that bugger has done to me? He exiled me because I revealed to the public that his Messalina of a daughter was a whore!"

That earned Voltaire a trip to the Bastille, where he stayed for thirteen months—admittedly in some comfort, since he had money.

Five years passed, and Voltaire was again on his way up the social ladder. Then, at a dinner party thrown by France's minister of war, he looked across the table and spotted Beauregard, the man who finked on him.

"I knew that spies were being paid," Voltaire sneered, "but I did not know until now that their reward was to dine at the minister's table."

The minister said nothing about it that night, but the next day, in broad daylight, Beauregard stopped Voltaire's carriage, dragged him out, and severely beat him.

Rather than hide until his bruises healed, Voltaire chose to flaunt his injuries and to complain. One of his least sympathetic listeners was none other than the regent. When Voltaire finished cataloging his woes, Philippe said simply, "You are a poet and you have been beaten. This is the order of things."

Voltaire's dealings with rulers were not always contentious. With King Frederick the Great of Prussia he was downright obsequious. When he wasn't gushing nonsense like "I prostrate myself before your scepter, your pen, your sword, your imagination, your justness of understanding and your universality," he was comparing the king to Apollo, Marcus Aurelius, and Caesar. Embarrassing, but it landed him a job in the king's court.

## Poe's "Pestilential Society of Literary Women" (1846)

Among his many talents, Edgar Allan Poe could snatch defeat from the jaws of victory, whether by making wild accusations against other writers (see "Poe Charges into the 'Longfellow Wars,'" on page 100), going on a bender, or pitching a fit and falling into it. One of those intemperate moments led to his expulsion from New York's literary society.

At the time, he was editor of the *Broadway Journal* and a visitor to Anne Lynch's salons, where ambitious literary women flocked to flirt with him. Far from being jealous, Poe's wife, Virginia, encouraged their attentions. Dying of consumption, she hoped that the women would help her Edgar stay sober.

One of them, the pretty Elizabeth Ellet, flattered Poe with her letters and attentions. In return, he printed her poems and praised her as "one of the most accomplished of our country-women." But Poe was flirting with disaster. Ellet had a fondness for rifling her friends' papers and spreading scandalous gossip.

There are contradictory stories behind the cause of their blowup. Ellet might have been jealous of Frances Osgood, another poet whom Poe had praised and exchanged flirtatious poems with. There is also the story that Ellet had entered the Poes' home and found them with Osgood, cackling over one of Ellet's notes.

For her part, Ellet claimed that Virginia had shown her a love letter to Poe from Osgood and asked her to help suppress the scandal. Ellet visited Osgood, chided her for her indiscretion, and persuaded her to send Lynch and journalist Margaret Fuller to Poe to get the letter back.

Poe exploded at Lynch and Fuller's request, calling them busybodies and snapping that Ellet should look to *her* letters instead.

This news set Ellet off, and she sent her brother, Colonel William Lummis, to get her letters back. Poe said he didn't have them; he was so overcome with remorse after the confrontation that he had packaged Ellet's letters and left them on her porch. Lummis didn't believe Poe and threatened to kill him.

Thoroughly frightened, Poe ran to his friend, Thomas Dunn English, and asked for a revolver to defend himself against Lummis. But English not only didn't believe Poe but said the letters probably never existed.

That got Poe riled up again, and here we have more dueling accounts. Poe claimed that he "gave E. a flogging." English said that he tried to fend off Poe and cut him with his seal ring. A witness who heard the ruckus entered the room and said he saw a drunken Poe "forced under the sofa, only his face being visible. English was punching Poe's face, and at every blow a seal ring on his finger cut Poe."

To complete the comedy, as they were being separated, Poe shouted—and I am not making this up—"Let him alone! I've got him just where I want him."

Poe apologized to Ellet and took to his bed until the scandal blew over, but his claim of temporary insanity cemented his reputation as unstable, if not deranged. Literary New York closed its doors to him, leaving him railing against "the pestilential society of literary women. They are a heartless, unnatural, venomous, dishonorable set, with no guiding principle but inordinate self-esteem."

# Thoreau the Firebug (1844)

Henry David Thoreau is known today as a conservationist and a philosopher, but to the residents of Concord, Massachusetts, he was better known as a crank and a "woods-burner."

It had been an exceptionally dry spring when he set off with Edward Hoar on a boat trip up the Sudbury River. They caught some fish and stopped on the shores of Fair Haven Bay for lunch. When a spark set the dead grass afire, they tried stamping it out. As the blaze raced out of control, Hoar took the boat downriver, while Thoreau raced through the woods to raise the alarm. By the time the townspeople could extinguish the blaze, more than three hundred acres of woods and fields were burned.

News of the fire hit the pages of the *Concord Freeman*, with Thoreau and Hoar branded as thoughtless and careless. They were shielded from prosecution only because Hoar's father, one of Concord's leading citizens, paid damages to the farmers.

Already regarded as an eccentric loafer, Thoreau's reputation hit a new low. But help was on the way. His friend Ralph Waldo Emerson had bought some land, and another friend encouraged Thoreau to "build yourself a hut, and there begin the grand process of devouring yourself alive." The next year, Thoreau moved to Walden Pond, where he would develop his philosophy about man's relationship to nature.

He even found a reason to justify his carelessness. "Who are these men who are said to be the owners of these woods, and how am I related to them?" he concluded. "I have set fire to the forest, but I have done no wrong therein."

Thoreau was also a tax evader, refusing for years to pay his poll tax over his opposition to the Mexican-American War and slavery. He was arrested and spent a night in jail but was released over his objections when his aunt paid his taxes. He used his experience to write "Civil Disobedience," an essay that would influence Mohandas Gandhi and Martin Luther King Jr.

# Horatio Alger's Unnatural Acts (1866)

A minister is caught molesting boys, and church officials send him away and shield him from prosecution.

A story ripped from today's headlines?

Think again. The year: 1866. The minister: Horatio Alger.

The precocious son of a Unitarian minister, Alger was intended for a bright future. He mastered Latin, Greek, and algebra at home. At Harvard, he wrote essays on medieval chivalry and Cervantes and was named Class Poet.

During the Civil War, he was too short (five foot, two inches), too nearsighted, and too asthmatic to enter the army. His sole contribution to the Union cause was *Frank's Campaign*, a novel in which a boy forms a combat unit while his father is away soldiering. Although the novel brought in some money, it wasn't enough to support Alger as a writer. So he entered the church and, with his father's help, became a minister at the Unitarian Church in Brewster, Massachusetts.

But within a year, unsavory rumors began to fly about the minister's curious behavior. Then, a boy delivering a book to Alger's room reported that the minister had locked the door and committed an "unnatural crime." An investigation followed. Two boys testified that Alger had molested them, too. Confronted with the evidence, Alger broke down, admitted that he had been "imprudent," and fled town.

The outraged congregation demanded Alger's arrest, but the American Unitarian Association hushed up the scandal and assured them that Alger would never work again as a minister.

Alger resettled in New York City. He lived in cheap apartments and befriended the poor boys who earned coins shining shoes and delivering newspapers and messages. He also turned to writing the more than 130 novels that would associate his name with boys who find success through luck and pluck.

Was he able to keep his hands to himself? A poem he wrote soon after his disgrace, "Friar Anselmo's Sin," hinted that Alger deeply wanted to atone. But after his death, his family burned all his papers and diaries, ensuring that Alger will keep his secrets forever.

> The lack of information about Alger was so complete that biographer Herbert Mayes resorted to fiction. In *Alger: A Biography Without a Hero*, Alger dreams of becoming president, acquires several mistresses, and adopts a Chinese boy who is killed by a runaway horse. Despite its excesses, *Alger* was accepted as fact until Mayes confessed in the late 1970s.

## Twain Feels the Flop Sweat (1877)

Budding humorists take note: Even Mark Twain faltered.

The occasion was the great dinner to honor John Greenleaf Whittier's seventieth birthday, and the guest list included the elder gods of American literature: Ralph Waldo Emerson, seventy-four; Henry Wadsworth Longfellow, seventy; and Oliver Wendell Holmes, sixty-eight.

While the other speakers delivered flowery, complimentary speeches, Twain decided to deflate the evening's pretensions, poke fun at himself, and honor the men at the same time. He had pulled off a similar stunt at a dinner honoring Ulysses S. Grant, so he felt confident he'd succeed again.

When it was his turn, he stood at the middle of the long table, amid the cigar smoke and clinking glasses, and told a story. As a young man tramping around California, he sought shelter one snowy night at a miner's cabin. After he identified himself, the miner grumbled that he was the "fourth littery man that has been here in twenty-four hours." Longfellow, Emerson, and Holmes had been there the previous night and spent the evening "strutting about, declaiming poetry, drinking and playing cards."

When a suspicious Twain suggested that the roustabouts were impostors and "not the gracious singers to whom we and the world pay loving reverence and homage," the miner delivered the punch line: "Ah! Impostors, were they? Are *you*?"

The response was a silence that one guest described as "weighing many tons to the square inch." Twain's attempt at self-satire was an epic fail.

The newspapers roasted Twain for portraying these noble litterateurs as slovenly, drunken roustabouts. He sent anxious apologies to the men, and Holmes and Longfellow responded with forgiving notes. But Emerson's daughter Ellen was made of sterner stuff, and you could hear the condescension dripping in her reply:

> We were disappointed. We have liked almost everything we have seen over Mark Twain's signature. . . . Therefore when we read this speech it was a real disappointment. I said to my brother that it didn't seem good or funny, and he said, "No it was unfortunate. Still some of those quotations were very good," and he gave them with relish and my Father laughed, though never having seen a [playing] card in his life, he couldn't understand [the reference] like his children.

Retelling the story nearly three decades later, Twain could still feel the heat of humiliation.

## Mencken Gets Played (1934)

Few people ever got the better of H. L. Mencken in a battle of wits. One of them was President Franklin D. Roosevelt, who had a little help from Mencken himself.

They clashed at that playground of Washington's press corps, the Gridiron Club. Every year, the club throws a dinner for the politicians featuring satirical speeches and skits and an address by the president, with everything off the record.

Mencken was there to speak, and he was looking forward to a convivial night. Before the dinner, Roosevelt called Mencken over to his wheelchair for a chat. Although Mencken had skewered "the imbecility of the New Deal" in print, he readily agreed to Roosevelt's promise to sheathe their claws for the night.

Mencken kept his promise. Roosevelt did not.

The president began his speech by patting himself on the back, saying Mencken's mildness meant his administration's policies "must be pretty good after all." Then, turning on his patrician tone, he lashed out at American journalism:

> There are managing editors in the United States, and scores of them, who have never heard of Kant or Johannes Muller and never read the Constitution of the United States; there are city editors who do not know what a symphony is, or a streptococcus, or the Statute of Frauds; there are reporters by the thousand who could not pass the entrance examination for Harvard or Tuskegee, or even Yale. It is this vast and militant ignorance, this widespread and fathomless prejudice against intelligence, that makes American journalism so pathetically feeble and vulgar, and so generally disreputable.

Then, with the room's nerves stretched taut, Roosevelt announced that he was quoting an essay by "my old friend, Henry Mencken," and the journalists exploded with laughter and cheers.

Mencken turned red. To Roosevelt, he said only, "Fair shooting." Privately, he seethed: "I'll get that son of a bitch."

Roosevelt was sanguine: "I felt in view of all the amusing but cynically rough things which Henry had said in print for twenty years, he was entitled to ten minutes of comeback."

**Mencken's hatred for Roosevelt was lifelong. Shortly before his disabling stroke, he was asked if he really disliked FDR as much as he wrote. "Every bit of it," he replied. "In my book that man was an unmitigated S.O.B. He was an S.O.B. in his public life and an S.O.B. in his private life."**

## Robert Frost Plays with Fire (1938)

While poet Robert Frost presented himself publicly as a crusty farmer-poet, there was a reason his friends privately called him Yahweh: He was a jealous god who brooked no rivals.

His friends were worried when he agreed to attend the renowned Bread Loaf Writers' Conference in Middlebury, Vermont. If anyone could dampen Frost's prima donna attitude, it was his wife, Elinor. But five months before the conference, she had died unexpectedly. Without his wife of forty-three years, one friend noted, Frost was "a great and powerful engine without the control of its flywheel."

Things were fine at first. Playing the avuncular New England poet, Frost lectured in the fields, signed copies of his books, and dispensed wisdom in the parlor of the Bread Loaf Inn.

That changed the night the attendees gathered in Treman Cottage to hear poet Archibald MacLeish. Frost was there, sitting in the back, curling and uncurling some papers he had found. As MacLeish read, Frost began heckling him.

"Archie's poems all have the same *tune*," he said in a whisper that could be heard in New York. As MacLeish read his single-sentence poem "You, Andrew Marvell," smoke curled from the back of the room. The audience turned and saw Frost beating out a small fire he had "accidentally" set. It took some time before the smoke could be cleared and the reading continued.

Meeting his fans afterward, MacLeish was asked to read from one of his radio plays. But Frost, fuming on the periphery, baited MacLeish with wisecracks and barbed comments. Finally, Bernard DeVoto, a scholar and friend of Frost, called out, "For God's sake, Robert, let him read!" Frost didn't respond, but within a few minutes, he managed to take offense at a comment and left in anger.

While MacLeish forgave Frost, DeVoto could not. "You're a good poet, Robert," DeVoto told him, "but you're a bad man."


## Jacqueline Susann Throws a Party (1969)

After *Valley of the Dolls* smashed sales records, expectations were high for Jacqueline Susann's follow-up, *The Love Machine*. As always, Jackie and her husband, Irving Mansfield, planned the publicity campaign down to the smallest detail, including the launch parties, for which she laid down a law—"no cripples"—explaining they'd only depress people.

The campaign would climax with a party at the American Booksellers Convention in Washington, DC. There, five hundred booksellers would enjoy a fabulous candlelight dinner, cocktails, and an orchestra. They would also get trinkets, such as rings, tie clasps, pendants, and cuff links featuring the ankh, the ancient Egyptian symbol of eternal life, which plays a role in the novel.

The trouble started at the receiving line. After Jackie greeted each guest by name, they were handed a Love Machine cocktail, a big tumbler filled with curaçao, Pernod, and vodka served over crushed ice and fruit. While one guest described it as "a liquid laxative," it was also sneakily potent.

Soon, five hundred drunken booksellers were making merry. Horseplay abounded as they flew paper airplanes made out of the publicity material and set fire to the chic Italian biscuit wrappers. As the pretty papers floated to the ceiling and threatened to set the ballroom on fire, dinner was hastily served.

Unfortunately, the menu consisted mostly of flambé dishes, chosen by Jackie for their drama. As she gamely table-hopped, she had to shield her wig from being flambéd as well.

Finally, there was a fanfare, and a spotlight picked out four waiters at the top of the staircase. They descended, bearing a giant cake shaped, of course, like the book. As the inebriated booksellers rose unsteadily and applauded, *The Love Machine* theme was played, and the cake was carried to Jackie.

Before it could reach its destination, a publicist slipped and fell into it.

Fortunately, the novel went over better than the book party.

It is not surprising that one critic who didn't like *Valley of the Dolls* was feminist Gloria Steinem, who described it as "for the reader who has put away comic books, but isn't ready yet for editorials in the *Daily News*."

# Public Pratfalls

- When English bookseller Edmund Curll announced he would republish a poem Alexander Pope published anonymously under his name, the poet vowed revenge. He met Curll at a tavern and secretly spiked his drink with an emetic. The bookseller barely made it home before he fell into convulsive vomiting. Pope crowed over his victory, but Curll published anyway.

- For seven years, Samuel Johnson toiled on his dictionary while his patron, Lord Chesterfield, gave him £10 and otherwise ignored him. When Chesterfield praised the published work in 1755, Johnson sent him a biting letter, asking "Is not a patron, my lord, one who looks with unconcern on a man struggling for life in the water and when he has reached ground encumbers him with help?" Instead of being abashed, Chesterfield would read aloud the choicest bits to his friends, exclaiming "this man has great powers."

- Oscar Wilde raised an eyebrow at a dinner party as his friend the author Frank Harris told a story that everyone knew he had stolen from Anatole France. In the embarrassed silence that followed, Wilde purred, "Frank, Anatole France would have *spoiled* that story."

- Sometimes, public embarrassments are worth it. When biographer Edmund Gosse encountered writer William Michael Rossetti and his daughter standing on a crowded London bus, he called out, "I understand you are an anarchist." "I must differentiate," Rossetti replied just as loud. "*I* am an atheist. My daughter is the anarchist." The outraged passengers fled, and the threesome took their seats.

# Grub Street

Ever since Gutenberg lost the rights to
his printing press, sharp dealings have
always been a part of publishing.

## Robert Burns Answers a Critic (1791)

The Scottish poet Robert Burns never let criticism slide off his back. One man who complained about his uncouthness and misuse of grammar received this blast in reply (translations of the italicized words follow):

Thou eunuch of language: thou Englishman, who never was south of the *Tweed*: thou servile echo of fashionable barbarisms: thou quack, vending the nostrums of empirical elocutions: thou marriage-maker between vowels and consonants, on the *Gretna-green* of caprice: thou cobbler, botching the flimsy socks of bombast oratory: thou blacksmith, hammering the rivets of absurdity: thou butcher, *imbruing* thy hands in the bowels of *orthography*: thou arch-heretic in pronunciation: thou pitch-pipe of affected emphasis: thou carpenter, mortising the awkward joints of jarring sentences: thou squeaking dissonance of cadence: thou pimp of gender: thou *Lyon Herald* to silly etymology: thou *antipode* of grammar: thou executioner of construction: thou brood of the speech-distracting builders of the Tower of Babel: thou lingual confusion worse confounded: thou *scape-gallows* from the land of syntax: thou scavenger of mood and tense: thou murderous *accoucheur* of infant learning: thou *ignus fatuus*, misleading the steps of benighted ignorance: thou *pickle-herring* in the puppet-show of nonsense: thou faithful recorder of barbarous idiom: thou persecutor of syllabication: thou baleful meteor, foretelling and facilitating the rapid approach of *Knox and Erebus*.

Translations: *Tweed* River, part of the border between Scotland and England; *Gretna-green*, Scottish border village where English couples eloped to marry without a waiting period; *imbruing*, to soak or stain; *orthography*, rules that translate speech into writing; *Lyon Herald*, a high official who acted for the Scottish king; *antipode*, opposite; *scape-gallows*, a person who deserved hanging; *accoucheur*, midwife; *ignus fatuus*, foolish fire, a phosphorescent swamp light that lures travelers into danger; *pickle-herring*, a clownish German puppet character; *Knox and Erebus*, Knox (actually Nyx) is the Greek goddess of the night; her brother, Erebus, is the personification of darkness in the underworld.

> **Burns also used his literary powers to make amends. When he had drunkenly offended the hostess at a party, he wrote in remorse "from the regions of Hell, amid the horrors of the damn'd" and begged "whisper to them that my errors, though great, were involuntary—that an intoxicated man is the vilest of beasts . . . that to be rude to a woman, when in my senses, was impossible with me!"**

## Poe's Poison Pen (1835)

Although known for his macabre stories and poems, Edgar Allan
Poe earned his living working for literary magazines, where his book
reviews could sting.

In an unsigned review in the *Southern Literary Messenger* of Laugh-
ton Osborn's *Confessions of a Poet*, a fictional memoir, Poe pointed out
that the novel's most remarkable feature "is the bad paper on which it
is printed, and the typographical ingenuity with which matter barely
enough for one volume has been spread over the pages of two." At the
end, when the poet vowed to kill himself, Poe advised him to carefully
check his pistol's priming, else "there would be no answering for the
consequences. We might even have a second series of the *Confessions*."

A decade later, after encountering Poe in New York City, Osborn
sent him a note asking about the review. Didn't Poe work for the
*Messenger* then? Did he write it?

Not at all, Poe replied. He never even worked for the magazine.
He didn't explain, of course, why his name was on the masthead.

"Your *Confessions of a Poet* I read many years ago with a very
profound sentiment of admiration for its author," Poe wrote. "I have
written warmly in its defence—"

It was an outright lie, but as an admirer of Poe's writings, Osborn
forgave him.

## Kafka Gets a Little Help from His Friends (1915)

In literature, as elsewhere, it's sometimes not what you know but
who you know. The story of Franz Kafka and the literary prize is a
perfect example.

On the surface, it was a heartwarming story Germany badly

needed during World War I. When wealthy playwright Carl Stern-heim was awarded the prestigious Fontane Prize, he generously refused the cash that accompanied it and asked that it go to an up-and-coming writer such as Kafka.

Kafka's publisher, Kurt Wolff & Co., was thrilled for its author, then known most for small pieces in Berlin's literary magazines. They were about to publish his novella *The Metamorphosis*, about a man who turns into a beetle, and the publicity—aided by five reviews praising the work—would boost Kafka's profile.

What the public didn't know, and Kafka, his publisher, and the prize's organizers weren't about to tell them, was the network of back-scratching that went on behind the scenes:

- The prize's judge that year, Franz Blei, was a novelist whose literary magazine was funded by Sternheim. He had even acted in one of Sternheim's plays.

- Blei not only knew Kafka but had published several of his pieces.

- In return, Kafka had generously praised Blei's work in various literary magazines.

- To top it all off, all three principals involved in the prize were either published by or working for Kurt Wolff & Co.

And those five rave reviews? Kafka's friends and friends of a friend.

---

At least Kafka found a good use for the money. Although he was already earning a good salary working for the state and living with his parents, the cash paid for several months at his favorite health spa, where men exercised in the nude and learned how to increase the size of their penises.

## Babbitt Does Stockholm (1930)

Winning the Nobel Prize for literature should be a capstone for a writer's career. For Sinclair Lewis, it represented his tombstone.

When the man with a heavy Swedish accent called Lewis and informed him he had won, Lewis thought it was a prank from his friend, Ferd Reyher. "Oh, yeah?" Lewis said. "You don't say! Listen, Ferd, I can say that better than you. Your Swedish accent's no good. I'll repeat it to you: 'You haf de Nobel Brize.'"

When he was convinced he had won, Lewis felt poleaxed. No American had won the Nobel for literature, and while his satirical novels of middle-class, middle-American—*Main Street*, *Babbitt*, and *Elmer Gantry*—were bestsellers, he wouldn't compare himself to Nobelists such as John Galsworthy and Rudyard Kipling.

Many in the literary world agreed. Conservatives and fundamentalists who called his satire anti-American were outraged. Liberals such as Sherwood Anderson thought he was too patriotic to be an artist. Over in Paris, Ernest Hemingway growled that James Joyce or Ezra Pound deserved it more, and newspaper editorialists added to his list Edith Wharton, Eugene O'Neill, and Willa Cather.

In England, the *New Statesman* wrote acidly that "previously none of the awards has been noticeably ridiculous."

While the barbs stung, worse was in store for Lewis. The America of the 1920s that he understood was fading after the 1929 stock market crash. Writers such as Hemingway and William Faulkner were taking literature deep into modernism.

Lewis seemed to know he was being left behind. In his Nobel speech, he observed that younger writers "are doing such passionate and authentic work that it makes me sick to see that I am a little too old to be one of them."

Lewis continued to write and publish until his death in 1951, but the Nobel effectively nailed shut his career.


## How Not to Write an Introduction (1931)

When Random House president Bennett Cerf republished *Sanctuary* for his Modern Library, he asked its author, William Faulkner, to add an introduction.

Big mistake.

Probably written while on one of his regular benders, Faulkner's essay contained a bizarre mix of facts and lies about when and how he wrote his books that would take his biographers years to unravel.

But Faulkner also did a masterful job of alienating potential readers. *Sanctuary*, he wrote, "is a cheap idea, because it was deliberately conceived to make money." He wrote it "trying to make out of it something which would not shame *The Sound and the Fury* and *As I Lay Dying* too much." He closed his sales pitch with "I hope you will buy it and tell your friends and I hope they will buy it too."

Faulkner ended his introduction with a note to his publisher, writing at the end of the manuscript in his tiny, neat script: "Fuck you Bennett."

That didn't make it into the book.


## Fitzgerald Plays Around (1934)

F. Scott Fitzgerald was in bad shape in 1934, with his best books behind him and his wife, Zelda, hospitalized for mental problems in Baltimore. In between visits to the hospital, he kept busy working on *Tender Is the Night* and other projects.

One idea was a revue of nonsensical short plays in the Grand Guignol style intended for Broadway. He worked on the idea with a seventeen-year-old high school student, Thomas Morfit, who had impressed Fitzgerald with his performance in Zelda's play *Scandalabra*.

Morfit, who later became known as comedian and game-show host Garry Moore, didn't know at the time that Fitzgerald was a novelist: "To me he was just a drunk. I'd show up at 7 o'clock, and he'd already be three-quarters in the bag." But he had nothing to lose. If the play went to Broadway, Morfit said, "I saw a chance to jump 16 steps in one leap."

It was a difficult collaboration. Fitzgerald would dictate dialogue, while Morfit took notes. Fitzgerald gave him colored pencils and told him to use a different one for each character. Morfit ignored the order, and when he was caught, Fitzgerald threw his arm toward the door and shouted, "Are you telling me how to write? Get out!"

When they weren't collaborating, Morfit would drive Fitzgerald around Baltimore. One night, when they approached the monument to Fitzgerald's namesake and relative, Francis Scott Key, Fitzgerald leapt from the car and hid in some bushes. Morfit stopped and asked what was up.

"Shhh!" Fitzgerald said. "I don't want Frank to see me this way." Morfit had to wave his handkerchief to "distract" the statue while Fitzgerald sneaked away.

They worked this way for four months until they needed a secretary. Morfit suggested using his pretty fifteen-year-old sister. Big mistake. Within a half hour, Fitzgerald was chasing her around the living room, and the Morfits fled the house. End of revue.

---

**Fitzgerald also "collaborated" with Zelda by using extracts from her journals verbatim in his books. He was so possessive of her that, when she wrote a novel, Fitzgerald accused her of stealing *his* material.**

---

## Anderson Pans His Critics (1946)

When a playwright receives a bad review, the best thing to do is let it pass and move on. After all, every great play has been pummeled in print: Shakespeare's *A Midsummer Night's Dream* ("The most insipid, ridiculous play that ever I saw in my life"—Samuel Pepys); Eugene O'Neill's *Strange Interlude* ("Rotten and morbid with decay"—James Agate); even *Fiddler on the Roof* ("No smash hit, no blockbuster"—*Variety*).

When Maxwell Anderson's *Truckline Café* opened on Broadway, it ran into a critical buzz saw. Despite Marlon Brando's presence, the reviews were vicious—"Downright unbearable," "the worst play I have seen," "Anderson hits his low with a dreadful new play"—and the play closed after thirteen days.

Anderson took the defeat hard, his daughter Hesper recalled, "then he did one of his famous slow burns." He called up the newspapers and, in full-page ads, reviewed the reviewers as fiercely as he was reviewed:

> It is an insult to our theater that there should be so many incompetents and irresponsibles among [the reviewers]. . . . Of late years all plays are passed on largely by a sort of Jukes family of journalism, who bring to the theatre nothing but their own hopelessness, recklessness and despair.

Jukes, by the way, was the pseudonym of New York hill families whose penchant for poverty, crime, and feeblemindedness were studied by sociologists.

# Norman Mailer Makes Lemonade (1955)

After great reviews for *The Naked and the Dead* and horrible ones for *Barbary Shore*, Norman Mailer had high hopes for his third novel, *The Deer Park*, a roman à clef about moral depravity in Hollywood.

But the reviews were mixed, with the negative reviews outweighing the good. Orville Prescott of the *New York Times* called it "nasty." The *San Francisco Chronicle* reviewer said, "Mailer has established a new par for the modern writing course: he has succeeded in making sex dull." The *Chicago Sun-Times* called it "sordid and crummy," and the *Cleveland News*, "the year's worst snake pit in fiction." Another opined: "This will set publishing back 25 years."

Mailer took the offensive. He thumbed his nose at the reviewers by taking out a half-page ad in the newly launched *Village Voice*, which Mailer had cofounded, and printed the worst blurbs he could find.

Harvey Shapiro, the editor of the *New York Times Magazine*, thought he was crazy. "I remember standing on the street corner with him and saying, 'Norman, writers don't act this way. It's not the dignified thing to do, it can only hurt you.'"

But he was wrong. The ad drew attention to Mailer, building an audience for his essays and nonfiction that would make him a provocative voice in American culture.

---

Mailer's use of obscene language stirred controversy, and he learned to game the editing process. For *An American Dream*, Mailer estimated that twelve swear words would make a particular passage effective, so he put in twenty, assuming that the editor would cut eight.

## Jacqueline Susann's Priorities (1963)

From her first book, Jacqueline Susann knew the value of self-promotion. She hustled booksellers, distributors, and journalists. She toured extensively. She was the first to visit the truck drivers who delivered her paperbacks at dawn, handing out Danish pastries and signing books for them.

So, the week after her first book, *Every Night, Josephine!* was published, she went to her publisher for a meeting and found the entire staff around the television set. President John F. Kennedy had been assassinated in Dallas.

Her response was characteristic: "Why the fuck does this have to happen to me? This is gonna ruin my tour."

## Olivia Goldsmith's Valentine (1996)

Novelist Olivia Goldsmith was passionate about her friends. She treated them almost as if they were lovers and showered them with praise and gifts. But, as befitted the author of *The First Wives Club*, in which spurned spouses took revenge on their husbands, she could be equally as passionate about rejection.

After working on several novels with Larry Ashmead, her editor at HarperCollins, she dedicated *The Bestseller* to him in fulsome terms: "To Larry Ashmead / Editor of Genius / Cultivator of Tomatoes. / Whose stories of writers, agents, editors, and publishers inspired, awed, and amused me. This is your book as much as it is mine." She also had included a large photo of him, grinning sheepishly at the camera.

But a year later, their relationship frayed over sex—that is, between the elderly characters in her next book.

*Marrying Mom* had "rather grotesque sex scenes . . . they had to rearrange their bellies to have sexual intercourse," Ashmead told *New York* magazine. "I asked her to take it out. That was the end of the relationship. She went out the door and never came back."

But she didn't forget her "Editor of Genius." On Valentine's Day, he found a bag of candy valentines at the front door from her. On each heart, the gooey sentiment had been painstakingly scratched out and replaced with loving thoughts such as "fuck you" and "screw you."

"It must have taken a lot of time," Ashmead said.

## Wretched Rejections

Every writer, no matter how talented, had to endure the slings and arrows of outrageous opinions, sometimes from equally notable authors:

- After submitting an article in 1889 to the *San Francisco Examiner*, Rudyard Kipling was informed, "I'm sorry, Mr. Kipling, but you just don't know how to use the English language."
- After seeing Anton Chekhov's *Uncle Vanya* in 1901, Leo Tolstoy told him, "You know I can't stand Shakespeare's plays, but yours are even worse."
- Gore Vidal had faint praise for Herman Wouk's *Winds of War* in 1973, saying, "This is not at all bad, except as prose."
- Sometimes, art is thicker than blood, such as when Kingsley Amis said of his son, "If I was reviewing Martin under a pseudonym, I would say he works too hard and it shows."

## · 4 ·

# Censors and Editors

Both want to fix your prose: one like a
mechanic, the other like a veterinarian.

## *Madame Bovary* Too Hot for France (1856)

With *Madame Bovary*, the French novelist Gustave Flaubert announced his intention to push the novel into uncharted territories. The magazine publisher in Paris who printed the opening chapters, however, was more worried about being arrested.

It was bad enough that Flaubert told the story of Emma's adultery without condemning her sin—as if unfulfilling affairs, financial fraud, and dying by poison weren't enough—but he had also written a sex scene that his publisher worried would anger the authorities.

The scene between Emma and Leon bears a close resemblance to a *Benny Hill* sketch. After meeting at a church, Leon bundles Emma into the back of a horse-drawn cab for a ride through the city. Every time the oblivious driver slows down or tries to stop, a voice inside the curtained cab calls out: "Go on!" "No, straight on!" and "Get on, will you?" As the exhausted horses are driven through the streets, Flaubert writes, the people stare "wonder stricken" at the curtained cab "tossing about like a vessel."

To avoid a possible arrest for immorality, the publisher dropped the "if the cab's a-rockin', don't come a-knockin'" scene. Alas, it was in vain. Flaubert and his publisher were hauled into police court and charged with committing an "outrage to public and religious morals." Fortunately for them, they were acquitted, and the publicity helped make *Madame Bovary* a success.

Despite that, Flaubert was still unhappy. "The success you obtain is never the kind you wanted," he grumbled. "It was the farcical bits in *Madame Bovary* that made it a success."

---

**Flaubert was a perfectionist when it came to writing, and it took him five years to finish *Madame Bovary*. Sometimes, he would take as long as a week to finish a single page.**

---

## Cabell Writes a Dirty Book (1919)

To be recognized as a great author, James Branch Cabell had to get banned.

Born into two of Virginia's first families, Cabell worked as a newspaper reporter before turning to fiction, but his elaborate historical romances made little impression in the market.

Then, in 1919, came *Jurgen: A Comedy of Justice*, in which a pawnbroker travels through history and searches for justice, engages in philosophical discussions about life, becomes an emperor, and—like *Star Trek*'s Captain Kirk—seduces numerous women, including the devil's wife.

Sounds like racy material, except that Cabell, every inch a Southern gentleman, was careful to use nothing but Victorian euphemisms about Jurgen wielding his magnificent scepter and thrusting sword and relied on fade-outs whenever passion arose. The erotic effect was so mild that *Jurgen* could be read to your grandmother without raising a blush.

But *Jurgen* aroused the fury of John S. Sumner of the New York Society for the Prevention of Vice. Describing ninety-five of *Jurgen*'s three-hundred-plus pages as "descriptive of scenes of lewdness and obscenity," Sumner banned the novel for being "offensive, lewd, lascivious and indecent" and indicted Cabell's publisher.

Two years later, while writers protested and literary bootleggers sold copies of the book for up to $30, the publisher was acquitted. Cabell became a bestselling author, but he wasn't grateful for Sumner's help. The revised *Jurgen* added a "lost" passage in which the Philistines put Jurgen on trial. The chief prosecutor was a large dung beetle.

## Mencken Battles Boston Censors (1926)

When H. L. Mencken bought the short story "Hatrack" for his *American Mercury* magazine, he was expecting to tweak a few puritanical noses, not risk jail.

Herbert Asbury's short story was about a cleaning lady in a small town who moonlighted as a prostitute, nicknamed "Hatrack" for her stick-like body. When her attempts to reform were rebuffed by her fellow churchgoers, she resumed her profession, ironically servicing her Catholic clients in the Protestant cemetery and the Protestants in the Catholic graveyard.

Because there were no descriptions of sexual activities, Mencken didn't expect trouble with the censors. But the Reverend J. Frank Chase of the New England Watch and Ward Society didn't find the story funny. He banned the magazine in Boston and threatened to arrest anyone who tried to sell a copy.

Mencken drew the line. Let one censor get away with it and more will follow. "I am against any further parlay with these sons of bitches," he told his publisher, Alfred Knopf. "Let us tackle them as soon as possible."

So at the appointed hour, Chase, the police, and the press gathered in Boston Common. Mencken displayed the *Mercury* issue, and Chase gave him a silver half dollar. Mencken delighted the crowd by biting it to make sure it wasn't counterfeit, sold Chase the magazine, and was arrested.

The showdown was orchestrated, but the consequences were serious. If found guilty, Mencken could sit in jail for up to two years. But after the judge heard the evidence and read the story, he ruled for the *Mercury*.

A much-relieved Mencken celebrated, posed for the newsreels, got a good night's sleep, and took the train back to New York . . . and discovered that Chase had gotten the postmaster general to ban the *Mercury* from the U.S. mails. It took several months to lift the ban, but not before Knopf had to pay $20,000 in legal fees, equal to about $190,000 today. It was an expensive victory for free speech.

> Mencken didn't always believe in fighting for free speech. When Theodore Dreiser wrote a play that was sure to be banned, Mencken was appalled. "Resisting with justice the imbecilities of the [censorious] Comstocks, you unconsciously fly to an extreme, and demand a freedom that is obviously impossible," he wrote. "I have no patience with impossibilities."

## The Censorious Librarian (1945)

When E. B. White's *Stuart Little* hit bookstores, it did so over the objections of a powerful librarian who wanted the little mouse exterminated.

As the first children's librarian for the New York Public Library, Anne Carroll Moore was a pioneer. She set aside a separate room for children to select and read books, created events such as story hours, and even allowed children to check out books on their own card. She gave lectures on children's literature and libraries would buy books on her word alone. Naturally, she decided which children's books the NYPL would buy, using a special rubber stamp—"Not recommended for purchase by expert"—on publishers' catalogs for works that fell short of her standards.

When she learned that the *New Yorker* writer was working on a children's book, she was eager to help. She begged to see the manuscript, offered praise for it in advance, and provided the essayist and editor with helpful advice about writing, all of which thoroughly irritated White. But when *Stuart Little* was ready, the publisher sent Moore—now retired—a prepublication galley.

Moore read the book and exploded. Instead of an improving tale for little minds, she found an unrealistic story of a mouse born to a human family. Interspecies miscegenation! She told the publisher the book "mustn't be published," and in her genteel way displayed the stick: "I fear *Stuart Little* will be very difficult to place in libraries and schools over the country."

"It is unnerving to be told you're bad for children," White wrote, "but I detected in Miss Moore's letter an assumption that there are rules governing the writing of juvenile literature—rules as inflexible as the rules for lawn tennis."

Moore got her successor at the library to buy only one copy, but keep it off the shelves. When White's editor learned of the exiled *Stuart*, she appealed to the library's director.

The director read the book and was furious. "Have those who talk about its abnormalities no imagination?" he wrote. He ended the ban. A year later, *Stuart Little* had sold more than a hundred thousand copies and was on its way to becoming a classic.

*Stuart Little* "got into the shelves of the Library all right," White wrote, "but I think he had to gnaw his way in."

## Slipping One Past the Editor (1947)

Editors have to keep a sharp eye to make sure authors don't slip anything too naughty into their stories. During the Golden Age of science fiction, at John W. Campbell's *Astounding Science Fiction* magazine, the editorial Cerberus was assistant Kay Tarrant. Blue pencil at the ready, Miss Tarrant, as she was known, kept her eye out for anything unsuitable in the manuscripts.

It is not surprising that the writers did their best to confound her. One who succeeded was George O. Smith, whose story "Rat Race" described a tomcat as "the original ball-bearing mousetrap."

But Smith wasn't the only science-fiction writer to sneak dubious material in their books. Stanley G. Weinbaum named a character in *A Martian Odyssey* Putz, the Yiddish word for penis. In Robert Heinlein's *Star Beast*, another penile reference was slipped in when it's revealed that the alien pet belonging to John Thomas Stuart XI is really royalty who considers the line of Stuarts to be her pets. This setup allowed Heinlein to get away with writing of the alien's "hobby of raising John Thomases."

## Piers Anthony's Revenge (1975)

Traditionally, writers have gotten along with editors as well as mice have gotten on with cats. Good editors such as Gordon Lish and Max Perkins can help make a writer's career, but many seem born imprinted with H. G. Wells's dictum that "no passion in the world is equal to the passion to alter someone else's draft."

But few writers have seen their prose run through the shredder as much as Piers Anthony over a quickie sci-fi potboiler.

In 1975, Anthony was contracted to write *But What of Earth?* a novel about the effects on earth of a massive migration to another

---

### Fahrenheit 451 in Real Life

Some censors preferred to let the flames do their work, even in the twentieth century:

- John Steinbeck's *Grapes of Wrath* caused controversy for its depiction of migrant workers fleeing the 1930s dust bowl Oklahoma for California. Farmers in Kern County, California, got the novel banned, and in 1939, publicized their displeasure by burning it. It was also burned twice in Steinbeck's hometown of Salinas, California.
- An Oklahoma City minister led a book burning in 1940 at a stadium, using materials stolen from the Progressive Bookstore, including works by Karl Marx and thirty-one copies of the U.S. Constitution.
- In 1973, the janitor at a North Dakota high school burned thirty-two copies of Kurt Vonnegut's *Slaughterhouse-Five* after the school board determined it was pornographic.

planet. He wrote it in two months and mailed it in, where it was accepted and the check was sent.

That's when trouble started. As the publication date neared, no proofs came. Anthony asked for them, repeatedly. In response, he received, not the proofs, but a brochure that promoted *But What of Earth?* which was supposedly written by two authors.

The editor told Anthony that he not only approved the collaboration but also the sharing of royalties. Didn't he remember? No, Anthony said, he was sure that he would remember agreeing to give half his income to a writer for a collaboration in which he didn't, technically, collaborate.

Then Anthony read the book. His story had been eviscerated. References to race, sex, and religion had been cut as was his main character's motive, rendering the novel pointless. "I was ashamed to have my name associated with this atrocity," he wrote.

Fortunately, the publisher was equally appalled. The editor was fired, and Anthony got his novel back, including the heavily edited manuscript, complete with the nasty comments of not one but four editors.

Then Anthony took his revenge. He republished *But What of Earth?* with its editorial notes and its long, strange trip to publication.

# 5

# Frauds and Hoaxes

Writers who tell lies for a living are
good at fooling people. Surprised?

## Swift Predicts a Death (1708)

When astrologer John Partridge defended science by attacking the
"infallible" Church of England, he hadn't reckoned on angering
ordained priest Jonathan Swift. Taking the name Isaac Bickerstaff,
Swift issued a list of predictions for 1708, including that Partridge
would be carried off by a raging fever at 11 p.m. on March 29.

On that day, Swift issued a black-framed elegy announcing not
only Partridge's death but also his confession before dying that he
was a fraud, making his predictions only for profit.

What happened next, according to Partridge, could have served
as the basis of a situation comedy. Early in the morning, the sexton
at the parish church called at Partridge's house, wanting to know
if the family wanted to order a funeral sermon. He was followed
by the undertaker inquiring about funeral plans. When Partridge
walked the streets, bemused Londoners gaped at him or told him he
resembled a certain dead astrologer.

Partridge issued another broadside telling his side of the story, but all of London seemed to prefer him dead. Swift's hoax had turned the astrologer into a punch line, and he was forced to cease publishing his almanac, leaving Swift to issue one last broadside:

### An Epitaph on Partridge

*Here, five Foot deep, lies on his Back,*
*A Cobbler, Starmonger, and Quack;*
*Who to the Stars in pure Good-will,*
*Does to his best look upward still.*
*Weep all you Customers that use*
*His Pills, his Almanacs, or Shoes;*
*And you that did your Fortunes seek,*
*Step to his Grave but once a Week:*
*This Earth which bears his Body's Print,*
*You'll find has so much Virtue in it,*
*That I durst pawn my Ears 'twill tell*
*Whatever concerns you full as well,*
*In Physic, Stolen Goods, or Love,*
*As he himself could, when above.*

## Mark Twain's Massacre (1863)

Before he broke into America's literary consciousness with his story of the jumping frog of Calaveras County, Mark Twain stepped over the line when newspaper readers didn't share his humor.

As a reporter at the *Virginia City Territorial Enterprise*, Twain wrote a story headlined "A Bloody Massacre Near Carson." According to the story, Philip Hopkins, the mild-mannered head of a large homestead between Empire City and Dutch Nick's, had ridden into town with his throat slit from ear to ear and holding a bloody scalp.

Hopkins died, and at his cabin, the sheriff found nearly the whole family slaughtered.

Twain piled on the gruesome description. Hopkins's wife had "her head split open and her right hand almost severed from the wrist." Six children had their brains dashed out. A daughter survived but "frightfully mutilated, and the knife with which her wounds had been inflicted still sticking in her side." Then Twain revealed that Hopkins went mad after losing his fortune investing in the stocks of crooked companies whose nefarious activities were covered up by the San Francisco newspapers.

It was a great story, but it was a hoax, designed to attack the newspapers and expose the stock-cooking schemes common among the mining companies.

Twain had used this ruse successfully before, but this time he miscalculated. Despite dropping hints that the story shouldn't be taken seriously, such as that Hopkins was known to be a bachelor, and Empire City and Dutch Nick's were two names for the same town, readers were revolted.

The next day, under the headline "I Take It All Back," Twain apologized, but the damage was done. Other newspapers picked up the story and lashed Twain for his supposed lack of ethics. It wasn't the first time that Twain overreached to make a point, and over his long life, it wouldn't be the last.

One of Twain's successful newspaper hoaxes poked fun at the mania for "petrified man" stories by reporting on one found sitting down against the mountainside. If you visualized his description of the man's hands— thumb to nose with the fingers spread—you'd realize he was cocking a snook. That so few readers didn't see the joke, Twain admitted, gave him a "soothing secret satisfaction."

# Upton Sinclair Fakes a Suicide (1902)

On June 9, 1902, the following obituary appeared in the *New York Times*:

> STIRLING—By suicide in the Hudson River, poet and man of genius, in the 22nd year of his age, the only son of Richard T. and Grace Stirling, deceased, of Chicago.

The heart-wringing notice touched many readers, so when the genius's *Journal of Arthur Stirling* appeared in February, reviewers paid attention.

Stirling's private thoughts were a mix of poetry and despair. He lamented living "in this seething hell of selfishness, this orgy of folly" and wrote of seeing his soul as a bubble, "whirling over a stormy sea; glorious with the rainbow hues it was, but perilous, abandoned." But there were some lighter moments, such as when Stirling experimented with eating raw eggs: "The experiment was not a success. You taste raw egg all day."

*The Journal* caused a brief stir upon publication, but a greater one later when it was revealed to be a hoax. An impoverished Upton Sinclair, reduced to writing dime novels and playing poker to make ends meet, got a reporter friend at the *Times* to plant the obituary in an attempt to draw attention to his work.

But the hoax had a more profound effect on Sinclair's career than he expected. Through it, he met George Herron, a wealthy socialist who became Sinclair's financial backer. This would lead to the publication four years later of *The Jungle*, Sinclair's muckraking attack on the meatpacking industry. The neglected genius became noticed at last.

## Virginia Woolf Punks the Royal Navy (1910)

It was a cool February day when Virginia Stephens, then eighteen and two years before becoming Mrs. Leonard Woolf, dressed up for a special outing: caftan, turban, false beard, and a healthy dollop of blackface. At the top of her to-do list that day: portray a royal Abyssinian and prank the flagship of the Royal Navy, the HMS *Dreadnought*.

Inveterate prankster Horace Cole had organized the stunt. He recruited a few friends, including future Bloomsbury painter Duncan Grant and Virginia's brother, Adrian, but when several people dropped out, Adrian talked Virginia into portraying the emperor's crown prince. With the help of theatrical costumes and beards, there would be four "Abyssinians" in all, plus Adrian playing an interpreter and Cole an official from the Foreign Office.

They sent a telegram to the ship, signed with the name of an Admiralty official, and convinced the railroad to provide a special coach for the trip to Weymouth. At the port, they were met by a ship's officer who escorted them by boat to the *Dreadnought*. As they neared the ship, the sailors stood at attention along the side of the ship and the band performed the national anthem . . . of Zanzibar. Lacking an Abyssinian flag and music, the British Navy made do.

For forty minutes, the party of six were given a grand tour of the battleship. They talked among themselves in a mix of Swahili and Latin tags from Virgil and Horace, and at every new British marvel, cried out "Bunga bunga!" Everyone agreed that it was a successful diplomatic mission.

Then news of the hoax hit the newspapers and torpedoed the navy's pride. A high navy official had to explain to Parliament how it happened. Children not only taunted sailors in the street with cries of "bunga bunga" but also the real, and no doubt puzzled, emperor of Abyssinia when he visited England weeks later. Reporters sought out Virginia for an interview and described her as "very good looking, with classical features."

Eventually, the uproar died down, and apologies were accepted all around. The navy's honor was restored when Cole and Grant were "punished" with ceremonial canings on their buttocks. Virginia was not only enormously amused at successfully passing as a man but learned something about masculine pride and honor that she would use in her fiction.

## Henry Miller Self-Publishes (1924)

When Henry and June Miller were broke and living in Brooklyn, they hit on a scheme to make money. Watching out-of-towners walk the streets of Greenwich Village, with its colorful artists, writers, drifters, and bohemians, they concluded that the tourists needed souvenirs.

Henry decided he would write a prose poem of about 250 words, get it etched on copper plates, run off a couple hundred of them, and sell them to the "thrillagers." It was an audacious scheme. The prospect of getting customers to pay for several paragraphs of sterling prose by an unknown writer seemed, at best, optimistic.

When the scheme failed, the Millers came up with an alternative. Before they were married, June had worked as a taxi dancer, flirting with men for money. So, under the pen name of June E. Mansfield, she concocted a story about being a struggling single woman with an invalid mother at home and found plenty of men who, hoping for more, were willing to buy her prints. Some of them might even have read them.

One of June's customers, a joke writer for *New Yorker* artist Peter Arno by the name of Roland Freedman, became infatuated with her.

He wrote her love letters and offered to support her while she wrote a novel and lived in Europe for six months. As June strung him along, Henry used the money to write his first novel, *Moloch*, and they laughed at Roland's belief that she could write prose such as "Keep your libraries. Keep your penal institutions. Keep your insane asylums. Give me beer."

> While living in Paris in the 1920s, Henry Miller wrote pamphlets advertising a new whorehouse, for which he was paid "a bottle of champagne and a free fuck in one of the Egyptian rooms." He also made ends meet by earning commissions for bringing in new customers.

## Richard Wright Commits Forgery (1927)

Long before his novels such as *Native Son* defined the African American experience in the segregated United States, it seemed that Richard Wright was destined for a life of menial work. He had dropped out of high school, and at age seventeen, was living in a rented room in Memphis, working odd jobs such as dishwasher and delivery boy.

But he had a thirst for knowledge and the wit to acquire it. He read voraciously, keeping a dictionary at hand to look up unfamiliar words.

Then, he encountered H. L. Mencken when he read a newspaper editorial attacking the iconoclastic writer. Anyone who upset the white establishment was worth pursuing, Wright decided, so he borrowed *Prejudices* and *A Book of Prefaces* from the public library.

In his memoir, *Black Boy*, Wright describes his shock at reading Mencken's assault on American hypocrisies: "I pictured the man as a raging demon, slashing with his pen, consumed with hate, denouncing everything American, extolling everything European or German, laughing at the weaknesses of people, mocking God, authority."

*Prefaces* directed him toward the realist writers such as Sinclair Lewis and Theodore Dreiser. "Could words be weapons?" Wright reflected. "Well, yes, for here they were. Then, maybe, perhaps, I could use them as a weapon?"

To get Mencken's books, Wright had resorted to forgery. The library was for whites only, so he borrowed a card from a white friend and showed up at the front desk with this note:

Dear madam: Will you please let this nigger boy have some books by H. L. Mencken?

By pretending to act as a delivery boy, Wright learned about the writers who would change his life. By the end of the year, he had left the South for Chicago, better-paying work, and the writer's life.

## Ern Malley: The Poet Who Never Was (1943)

Meet Ern Malley, who didn't let a little thing like nonexistence prevent him from becoming one of Australia's greatest modernist poets.

Malley was created as an instrument of revenge by poets James McAuley and Harold Stewart. They were serving in the Australian army during World War II, and shared an intense dislike both of modern poetry and, in particular, one of its proponents: Max Harris, the editor of the literary journal *Angry Penguins*.

So, while doing their part to keep Melbourne safe from the Japanese, McAuley and Stewart decided to hoax Harris and modernism. In an afternoon, they composed the complete works of Ernest Lalor

Malley: sixteen poems, cobbled from the materials on their desks, obscure enough to evade understanding, yet sincere enough to fool Harris.

They gave Malley an attractively tragic—and difficult to trace— biography that ended with his death at twenty-five of Graves' disease. They also created Ethel, Ern's sister and sole survivor, who wrote to Harris and entrusted him with *The Darkening Ecliptic*, Malley's sole manuscript.

Harris thought he had found some hot stuff. Calling Malley "one of the most outstanding poets we have produced," he devoted the next issue of *Angry Penguins* to Malley.

For a year, gossip about the hoax percolated through Australia's small literary world. It wasn't until June 1944 that newspapers revealed the illusionary genius of Ern Malley.

Harris was shocked and humiliated, but he insisted that the poems had merit. One can hardly blame him for not catching lines like "that a poet may not exist . . . yet I know I shall be raised up / on the vertical banners of praise" as clues from the hoaxers that Ern Malley didn't exist.

One reason the hoax succeeded was that the first poem was particularly good. Once the hook was set, it was easy for Harris to overlook nonsensical lines, such as these taken from a mosquito-eradication manual: "Swamps, marshes, borrow-pits and other / areas of stagnant water serve / As breeding-grounds."

Meanwhile, police in Adelaide, where *Angry Penguins* was printed, were on the case. The suggestive words and images in the poems led to Harris's arrest for publishing obscenity. (McAuley, Stewart, and the other owners and editors of the magazine were beyond the local law's jurisdiction.) Despite the trial's farcical moments—one police officer testified that he didn't know the meaning of the word "incestuous," but "I think there is a suggestion of indecency about it"—Harris was found guilty and fined £5.

But Ern Malley lives on as one of Australia's great poets, with his complete works found in *The Bloodaxe Book of Modern Australian Poetry*. In 2003, Booker Prize–winning author Peter Carey closed the circle by publishing *My Life as a Fake*, creating a fictional biography about a man who never existed in the first place.

Ethel would be so proud.

---

**For his final exam at Brooklyn College, poet John Ashbery would give his students a poem by Malley and one by Geoffrey Hill and ask them to spot the fake. Half picked Hill.**

---

## The Howard Hughes Affair (1972)

Clifford Irving's plan to scam the public with a bogus biography would have worked if it weren't for that meddling billionaire.

A longtime novelist, Irving ran into trouble when his publisher rejected his latest work and he needed money fast. So, with writer Richard Suskind, he decided to fake an autobiography of reclusive industrialist, aviator, and filmmaker Howard Hughes.

Hughes's life could have come out of a Harold Robbins's potboiler (in fact, Robbins did just that for *The Carpetbaggers*). He built his father's company into a worldwide conglomerate that made him a billionaire. He plowed his money into making movies and dated scads of women, including Ava Gardner, Katharine Hepburn, and Bette Davis. He set flying records, built the world's largest flying boat, and nearly died when his test plane crashed in Beverly Hills. But for fifteen years, Hughes had been living in a J. D. Salinger–like seclusion so complete that some thought he was dead. Irving and Suskind bet that, even if Hughes were alive, he wouldn't risk coming out of hiding to denounce them.

Using counterfeit letters, the writers convinced McGraw-Hill that Hughes was cooperating with the autobiography, and negotiated a $500,000 advance that was later boosted to over $1 million. Irving's research at the Library of Congress turned up Hughes's letters and tape-recordings of his voice that he used to fake interview tapes. A former Hughes associate supplied his memoir of working with Hughes, and an investigative reporter's unpublished manuscript gave them more material.

Meanwhile, news of the book rocked the literary world and interest was sky-high. But two months before publication, Hughes blew

## Flimflam Authors

Literary history is full of writers willing to tell a stretcher to advance their careers, make a point, or promote themselves:

- The first edition of *Leaves of Grass* in 1855 was heralded with anonymous reviews praising this "transcendent and new" work and calling Walt Whitman "an American bard." Naturally, the reviews were written by Whitman.
- In 1877, early in his career, Hoosier poet James Whitcomb Riley printed a poem in the newspaper he worked for, claiming it was by Edgar Allan Poe. He ginned up a feud by planting anonymous articles in a rival paper claiming the poem was a hoax. When more newspapers published the poem, he was exposed, and Riley was fired.
- As a book reviewer for the *Yorkshire Post*, Anthony Burgess wrote a review in 1963, partly of praise, partly a warning of its contents, of Joseph Kell's novel *Inside Mr. Enderby*. Burgess knew its author well, for it was he. The *Post*'s literary editor was not amused and dismissed Burgess.

the whistle. He spoke by phone to seven reporters who had known him when he was a public figure. At the televised press conference, he denounced Irving as a fraud and the book a fake. "I only wish I were still in the movie business," he said. "Because I don't remember any script as wild or as stretching the imagination as this yarn has turned out to be."

Irving denied it, but then his wife, Edith, was identified as the woman who deposited a check made out to "H. R. Hughes" in the couple's Swiss bank account. Convicted of fraud and other charges, the Irvings and Suskind received jail time.

But the story didn't end there. Irving not only saw his "autobiography" made available on the Internet, but his account of the affair, *The Hoax*, was made into a movie starring Richard Gere.

Sometimes, crime pays.

# 6

# Money

"No man but a blockhead ever wrote,
except for money," but a writer who is his
own manager has a fool for a client.

## Much Ado About Shakespeare's Taxes (1597)

We know very little about Shakespeare, except that he was as much a businessman as an artist. Over the course of his life, the son of a Stratford glove maker became part-owner of the Globe Theatre, invested in commodities, and became one of the largest property owners in his hometown.

Shakespeare also loaned money at interest. When fellow Stratfordian Richard Quiney was in London on behalf of the village and ran short, he sent Shakespeare a letter seeking help. Addressing him as "Loving countryman," he asked for £30—about £720 or $1,440 today—a substantial sum for the time.

During that period, Shakespeare was also apparently cutting corners on his taxes. His name shows up on a legal document listing tax evaders who failed to pay 5 shillings. The next year, the authorities in London's Shoreditch borough recorded that Will failed to pay a 13-shilling, 4-pence tax on goods valued at £5.

It wasn't as if he couldn't afford to pay. He earned twice that amount in a week from his work in the theater and his share in the Lord Chamberlain's Men. He had even purchased the second-largest house in Stratford that year.

So, with Shoreditch's equivalent of the IRS hot on his heels, Shakespeare fled across the river, where his company built the Globe Theatre. But the wheels of justice and tax collection grind slow but fine. By 1599, they had caught up with Will, and this time, he paid up.

That still left the earlier bill for 5 shillings. We hope he paid it—one shudders to think of the interest on 5 shillings over four hundred years.

## Sheridan Gets the Trots (1780s)

The playwright Richard Sheridan was known for his radiant wit and ability to think in a crisis. His quickness of tongue was equal to his slowness in paying his bills, and he would regularly run up debts of thousands of pounds. Worse, he rarely opened letters, even those containing bank drafts, preferring to leave them stacked on a table in the front hall, which his theatrical manager dubbed the "funeral pile."

His long-suffering wife, Elizabeth (whose courtship is described in "Richard Sheridan Plots an Elopement," on page 165), was resigned to his idiosyncrasy: "You know Dick hardly ever reads his own letters: so that it [might] be in the bottomless pit for any good I am ever likely to reap by it."

As a result, he was constantly beset by his creditors. When one of them caught up to Sheridan during his stroll on the Mall in London, the playwright, instead of fleeing, paused.

"Oh, that's a beautiful mare you are on," he said.

"D'ye think so?"

"Yes, indeed, how does she trot?"

The creditor demonstrated by putting her into a full trotting pace, and that's when Sheridan took the opportunity to trot off himself.

---

**Sheridan's power of persuasion was accentuated by his appearance, but only to a point. Lord Byron expressed it best: "the upper part of Sheridan's face was that of a god—a forehead most expressive, an eye of peculiar brilliancy and fixity, but below—he showed the satyr."**

---

## Walter Scott Hits the Skids (1826)

Scotsmen are notorious for being frugal, but that stereotype didn't apply to Sir Walter Scott, the patron saint of Scottish literature. He invested heavily in renovating his estate, Abbotsford, and filling it with curios. Some of the money came from his historical novels such as *Ivanhoe*, but he made much more as a secret partner in John Ballantyne and Co., the publishing house that printed them.

But behind the scenes, John Ballantyne was a nineteenth-century Enron. Scott published unprofitable books by friends and writers he admired. He also used the company's cash flow to pay for renovations to Abbotsford and drew advances for books that would not be written for years. Meanwhile, bankers and investors poured money into the company believing that Scott's estate was a company asset. (It wasn't. Scott had signed it over to his son but neglected to tell his partners.)

When a financial crisis hit England, the company couldn't repay a £1,000 loan on time, and worried bankers cut off its credit. The house of cards collapsed, bankrupting the company and leaving Scott owing more than £121,000—the equivalent of more than £8 million today.

But Scott's reputation was so high that he was forgiven. Friends and admirers offered to pay off the debt. Scott's Scotch pride revolted at accepting charity, and he said, "No! This right hand shall work it all off!"

Scott devoted the rest of his life to writing his way out of debt, sometimes spending all day at his desk and suffering from depression and headaches. His publishers and doctors warned him that he was risking his health, but he replied, "As for bidding me not work, Molly might as well put the kettle on the fire and say, 'Now, don't boil.'"

Four years later, he suffered the first of four strokes that would eventually kill him at age sixty-one. The year after his death, his estate cleared the last of his debts.

## The Devil and Theodore Dreiser (1926)

When publisher Horace Liveright proposed selling the movie rights to Theodore Dreiser's *An American Tragedy*, the author thought he was nuts. Why would Hollywood be interested in the story of a man who tries to kill his pregnant girlfriend and is convicted of murder?

But Liveright was persistent. He proposed a deal in which Dreiser would get the first $50,000 and half of the rest. Dreiser thought he couldn't do it but agreed anyway.

After his return from Hollywood, Liveright took his employee, Bennett Cerf, and Dreiser to lunch at the Ritz-Carlton Hotel. There, as their coffee was being served, he broke the news that he'd sold the rights for $85,000.

Dreiser was delighted, and while he was figuring out how he would spend $85,000, Liveright reminded him of the deal: Dreiser would get $67,500, Liveright $17,500.

Dreiser was furious and shouted, "Do you mean you're going

to take my money?" When a waiter brought the coffee to the table, Dreiser grabbed a cup, threw it in Liveright's face, and stomped out.

"Bennett, let this be a lesson to you," Liveright told the future publisher as he mopped his shirtfront. "Every author is a son of a bitch."

---

Before he was a writer, Theodore Dreiser was a newspaper reporter for the *St. Louis Globe-Democrat*. Although highly regarded as a reporter, he sometimes cut corners. He had to resign when he faked a review of a performance that had been canceled.

---

## A Deal on the Wild Side (1957)

American novelist Nelson Algren's attitude toward money was paradoxical. On the one hand, he wanted it and complained bitterly when he felt he didn't get enough. Of his novel *The Man with the Golden Arm*, he complained, "I wrote a big American novel. Where's the hi-fi? Where's the stereo?"

But when it came to negotiating deals, Algren was his own worst enemy. When producer Joseph Lebworth offered him $25,000 for the movie rights to his novel *A Walk on the Wild Side*, Algren bypassed his agent (and her cut of the fee) and asked two theatrical producers for advice. They read the contract and concluded that Lebworth was trying to buy the rights cheap to resell them. Don't sign, they said. Even Algren's financial adviser and longtime friend, Art Shay, told him not to sign.

But Algren was broke and the temptation was too great, and Algren signed the contract. For weeks, he kept the check on his kitchen table, letting it get food stained, until he decided he was going to be a landlord. He cashed the check and, with a paper bag full of money, bought a Chicago apartment building. But when he realized he was unsuited for the job, he sold the building back to the

## Opportunity Knocks

- Mark Twain's failures in business were nearly as great as his successes in literature. His worst decision was to invest in a mechanical typesetting machine that would have revolutionized printing if it had worked. Instead, Twain went broke, losing nearly $5 million in today's dollars. In 1890, he ruefully noted that, while he remained friends with the inventor, James Paige, "he knows perfectly well that if I had him in a steel trap I would shut out all human succor & watch that trap until he died."
- William Faulkner's move from Harcourt, Brace to his new publisher was a welcome change, but something had to be done about his anemic sales. His next novel, *Sanctuary* (1931), promised to be controversial with its scenes of bootlegging, drunkenness, violence, and a rape involving a corncob. So, for $500 under the table, critic Alexander Woollcott devoted his popular *Town Crier* radio program to it, calling it a work of genius. *Sanctuary* became a bestseller.
- Hilaire Belloc and G. K. Chesterton were close friends who worked together on so many causes that they were nicknamed "the Chesterbelloc." But Belloc also loved making money; when asked why, he would reply "because my children are howling for pearls and caviar." When Chesterton died in 1936, Belloc attended the service at London's Westminster Cathedral. During the Mass, he sold his "exclusive" thoughts about his friend to four newspapers.

real estate agent at a loss and gambled away the rest. Two months later, Algren was broke again.

As for Lebworth, Algren's advisers were right. He resold the film rights for $75,000 to producer Charles Feldman, who made the movie in 1962 starring Lawrence Harvey, Capucine, and a twenty-four-year-old Jane Fonda. Algren refused to watch the movie.

· PART TWO ·

# Off the Job

# 7

# Odd Jobs

Believe it or not, writing wasn't always a
lucrative profession. Sometimes, you had
to do real work.

## Audubon Paints a Rare Bird (1821)

After he went bankrupt in the Panic of 1819, painter John James
Audubon left his family in Kentucky and traveled to New Orleans
to find work while researching birds for his longtime project *Birds
of America.*

Audubon was so poor that when his pocket was picked, the thief
got only his letters of introduction to New Orleans society. But he
persevered and landed several drawing commissions. Then, a veiled
woman opened a strange chapter in his life.

She had recognized him as the bird painter and asked him to meet
her at a particular address. There, she threw back her veil, revealing
what he described as "one of the most beautiful faces I ever saw." She
gave him a cordial, which he nervously drank. She peppered him
with questions about himself, his work, and his wife. Then, after
extracting a promise never to reveal her name and address, asked if
he would execute a portrait of her . . . without plumage.

Nude, that is.

"Had I been shot with a 48-pounder through my heart," he wrote to his no-doubt nonplussed wife, "my articulating powers could not have been more suddenly stopped."

Every day, for several hours, Audubon "had the pleasure of this beautiful woman's company about one hour naked and two talking on different subjects." She also corrected the errors in his work, criticized his difficulty handling foreshortening, and even worked on the picture when he was away.

Two weeks later, the painting was finished. She rewarded him with an expensive hunting rifle and composed the inscription engraved on the barrel: "Do not refuse this gift from a friend who is in your debt; may its goodness equal yours." As for the identity of the woman or the painting, neither has surfaced.

# Emily Brontë, Teacher (1838)

During her short life, Emily Brontë left the family home in Haworth only twice: to travel to Brussels with her sister Charlotte and to Law Hill to begin an ill-fated attempt at teaching girls.

It was not a happy time. She was homesick for her beloved moors and, according to Charlotte, was worked like a dog: "Hard labour from six in the morning until near eleven at night, with only one half hour of exercise between—this is slavery. I fear she will never stand it."

Emily quickly discovered that she had no affinity for children, particularly when they misbehaved. At one point, she told them that she felt more affection for the school's mascot, a dog, than she did for them.

She lasted six months. The end came while she was leading her students on a nature walk and came across a boy kicking a hedgehog. Outraged, she cuffed him. The students told the headmistress, and when she asked Emily for an explanation, she responded by packing and leaving that same day.

## Konrad Korzeniowski Loses His Way (1878)

If you had asked Joseph Conrad about his life as a young apprentice seaman in Marseilles, he would have told you about the time he smuggled guns to help the pretender to the Spanish throne. If he was melancholy, he would have revealed his tragic romance with a Basque girl or the time he was wounded fighting a duel.

Great stuff, except most of it wasn't true.

Conrad—born Konrad Korzeniowski in Russian-occupied Poland and orphaned at age eleven—had come to France to avoid mandatory military service. He acquired a forged permit that allowed him to work on merchant ships. When he ran up debts, he'd telegram Uncle Bobrowski, his guardian, for help. Bobrowski always came through, usually with a lecture that Konrad should mend his ways. "I would have refused my own son outright after so many warnings," he'd say, "but to you, the child of my Sister, grandson of my mother, for once, but *only for once*, I forgive you."

Then, at age twenty-one, Konrad ran into serious trouble. He went bust investing his money on a smuggling venture to Spain (the royalty story was nonsense; he was importing consumer products to avoid taxes). He doubled down by gambling in Monte Carlo and went broke.

In despair, he staged a suicide attempt. He invited his creditor to tea, then shot himself in the chest. The bullet skittered across his ribs, leaving him wounded. The creditor called a doctor and telegrammed Uncle Bobrowski. He arrived after a three-day train trip from Kiev, settled the debts, and had a long talk with his nephew.

Konrad, his forgiving uncle wrote home, "is not a bad boy, only one who is extremely sensitive, conceited, reserved, and in addition excitable."

Then Konrad had to leave Marseilles after French officials

discovered his forged permit. He boarded a steamer for Lowestoft, England. There, Konrad Korzeniowski signed onto English ships, learned a new language, and eventually became Joseph Conrad.

> In 1923, Conrad visited America. While staying at an estate on Long Island, the caretaker prevented two fans—visiting late at night and fueled by alcohol—from performing a dance under his window. The admirers were Ring Lardner and F. Scott Fitzgerald.

## Rimbaud the Gun Runner (1885)

It's not often a poet turns from selling sonnets to selling weapons, but Arthur Rimbaud wasn't your typical poet.

By age twenty-one, after years of playing the bad boy of poetry—drinking and drugging, conducting his scandalous affair with the poet Paul Verlaine (see "Rimbaud: 'You Really Look Like a Dick!'" on page 192), and burning his bridges with patrons and friends—Rimbaud was exhausted. He swore off poetry and riotous living and turned to making money, working as a mercenary, construction foreman, and even circus manager.

When he washed up on the coast of East Africa by the Red Sea, he came up with a new scheme. King Menelik II of Shoa needed guns, and Rimbaud and his partners had acquired 2,040 rifles. True, they were forty years old and out of date for European armies, but Rimbaud and his cronies bet they could sell them in Africa for five times their worth.

But sealing the deal required delivering the guns to Shoa's capital, Entotto, four hundred miles inland, across bandit-infested desert wastelands. Illness carried off Rimbaud's two partners, and natives ripped off the caravan at every opportunity. In Entotto, Rimbaud sold the rifles, but for less than he expected. His late associates' creditors caught up with him, including one partner's native wife, and he had to pay them off.

He complained to his mother, "I have emerged from the deal with a 60 per cent loss on my capital, not to mention 21 months of atrocious exertions spent liquidating this wretched affair."

A busted venture. Or was it? Rimbaud's biographer, Graham Robb, combed through the records and found that the man who complained of making a pitiful 6,000 francs had actually deposited 16,000 francs in the bank—about $90,000 today.

"Rimbaud had abandoned poetry," Robb concluded, "but not fiction."

## Jack London Catches Gold Fever (1897)

When news reached San Francisco that gold had been discovered in Canada's Klondike, among those who saw an opportunity was a young Jack London. The twenty-one-year-old had already lived an adventurous life hunting seals in the Bering Sea and sailing a sloop, but this journey would test him like nothing before.

Jack and his brother-in-law sailed by steamship to Juneau. Unable to afford porters, they backpacked several thousand pounds of supplies, 150 pounds at a time, for twenty-five miles to the Yukon River. There, they built two twenty-seven-foot-long boats and headed downstream with six miners.

Winter had set in. Amid scenes of incredible beauty, they twice saw boats dumped in the rapids and men thrown into the freezing water to die. The worst of the journey was at Box Canyon, where the Yukon narrowed to eighty feet, creating treacherous rapids and up-thrusting waves. Faced with a two-day portage or a two-minute run, London and the miners voted to risk their lives on the river.

At one of the tillers, Jack bolstered his courage with several pulls of whiskey. As the boats hit the current, they shook and took on water. His bowman mistimed a thrust with his spar and fell to the deck. Jack threw himself on the tiller and cracked it. The boat veered toward the rock wall and tragedy. Only at the last minute did the current push it away, and they reached calmer waters.

At the goldfields, Jack and company hunkered down in an abandoned cabin and swapped stories until spring. But Jack's hardships had caught up with him. He developed scurvy, his gums turned black, and his front teeth fell out. Weak from hunger, he returned home. While he hadn't found gold, Jack mined his experiences for stories such as *The Call of the Wild* and *White Fang* that would turn him into a popular author.

> **London earned a fortune from writing, and he spent it nearly as quickly. Much went toward building his dream mansion, dubbed the Wolf House. Built from redwood on a massive stone foundation, it ate up $80,000, roughly $1.4 million today. Two weeks before it was finished, it accidentally caught fire and burned to the ground.**

## Faulkner Goes Postal (1924)

William Faulkner may have been one of America's greatest novelists, but he was a lousy postmaster.

For the twenty-four-year-old World War I veteran, running the post office at the University of Mississippi in Oxford should have been a snap: sort the letters, deliver the mail, maybe sell a few postage stamps.

Not Faulkner. He opened the post office when it suited him, and closed it when he wanted to go hunting or golfing. He'd trash the advertising circulars, university bulletins, and other mail he deemed junk and keep the magazines in the back for a few days for his friends to read in between bouts of mahjongg and bridge.

After three years and numerous complaints, the post office had enough. When his fate became clear, Faulkner resigned, but not before writing a note to his superiors:

> As long as I live under the capitalistic system I expect to have my life influenced by the demands of moneyed people. But I will be damned if I propose to be at the beck and call of every itinerant scoundrel who has two cents to invest in a postage stamp.

## Colette's Beauty Business (1932)

If ever there was a can't-miss business investment, it should have been Colette's beauty company.

After all, the writer was considered France's epitome of femininity, renowned for her looks, her scandalous affairs with both sexes, and her novels about relationships and love. And like any good provincial housewife, she had learned her mother's beauty secrets, and she would concoct her cold creams and lanolin pomades from her own recipes. She had also picked up some techniques that Arab women used, such as using leather hair curlers and shading their eyes with kohl, but she stopped at using necklaces of dried gazelle droppings.

Colette oversaw all aspects of setting up her salon. She spent days in a lab to create the formulas for her products. She worked with the designers on the look of the bottles and boxes, sketched a profile of herself for the labels, and chose for her logo a variation of her signature. She even convinced a friend to steal some Max Factor products so she could learn its secrets.

But Colette's quest to become the Parisian Mary Kay was a disaster. Because she hated to wear glasses in public, the results of her

---

# A Potpourri of Publications

Writers have always had to scramble to make a living, sometimes turning their talent for words in unexpected directions:

- When Walt Whitman was offered $125 to write a temperance novel, he did the job right. For three days, he downed gin cocktails and the occasional bottle of port and cranked out twenty thousand words a day. He thought *Franklin Evans, or the Inebriate* (1842) was "damned rot," but the book sold more than twenty thousand copies, more than any of his editions of *Leaves of Grass*.
- William Saroyan is known for his humorous, optimistic observations of humanity in *The Human Comedy* and the play *The Time of Your Life*, but he also left his mark on popular music. He cowrote with his cousin Ross Bagdasarian (who later created Alvin and the Chipmunks) "Come On-a My House," a dialect song in which a woman lures her paramour with candy and other enticements. Rosemary Clooney's version became a number one novelty hit in 1951.
- While Shirley Jackson is known more for her horror works such as *The Lottery*, she also published a short-story collection *Raising Demons* (1957). But instead of a book about the occult, Jackson was referring to her four children, anticipating Erma Bombeck by nearly a decade.

makeovers tended to look more like Picasso paintings, giving one actress friend an asymmetrical look that doubled her age.

Colette also combined an inability to flatter her customers with a writer's bluntness. Declaring that she was marketing her services to women with "a childish ignorance about what suits their faces" and "a timid fear of not being like everybody else," was not calculated to win her customers. When she advised a mother to style her daughter's hair with bangs, the mother protested, "That would be a waste. She has such a pretty forehead; why hide it?"

Colette shot back, "True, but I'm sure she also has a pretty arse, and you hide that."

Within two years, the business had failed.

# 8

# Crime and Punishment

Tangling with the law can land you
in the pen, but it can also inspire a
great work.

## Ben Jonson Escapes the Hangman (1598)

Over Ben Jonson's lifetime, the playwright was in and out of trouble with the authorities both on and off the stage. But one incident in particular could have cut his life short at twenty-six—before his greatest works were written.

It happened when Jonson was challenged to a duel, for reasons unknown, by Gabriel Spenser, a talented actor in Philip Henslowe's acting company. Despite fighting with a rapier ten inches shorter than Spenser's (or so Jonson, a notorious embellisher of stories, claimed later), Jonson ran Spenser through, killing him.

Jonson was charged with manslaughter, then punishable by hanging. But in court, Jonson pleaded guilty, called for a Bible, translated a brief passage from the Latin, and claimed "benefit of clergy." This legal loophole once allowed clergy to be tried only by ecclesiastical courts (in medieval times, the ability to read Latin was considered proof that you were ordained). Over time, the exception grew to encompass anyone literate, like Jonson.

While Jonson avoided the hangman's noose, he was ordered to forfeit his property and be branded on the thumb with the letter *T* to prevent him from again claiming the benefit. But the wily Jonson evaded the "Tyburn T" by bribing the jailer to brand him with cold steel.

Henslowe wasn't placated by losing a favored actor and took out his anger on Jonson by refusing to produce his next play. So *Every Man in His Humour*, considered Jonson's first great play, was performed by another company, including the actor and wannabe playwright, William Shakespeare.

## The Fall and Rise of Daniel Defoe (1703)

On the morning of July 29, in his cell at Newgate prison, the future novelist Daniel Defoe had good cause to wonder if he would live to see the next day. For writing an essay that fooled too many powerful people, he would stand for three days in the pillory, exposed to the rage of a London mob.

It was a serious sentence. Locked in the stocks and unable to defend himself, the miscreant could expect beatings and showers of rocks, garbage, and dead cats. Some prisoners ended up mutilated or traumatized. Others died.

Defoe's crime was writing a pamphlet that satirized the attitude toward Dissenters, those who refused to accept the state-sanctioned Church of England. Defoe suggested solving the problem by killing them. After all, Defoe reasoned, if Moses had slain thousands of Israelites who had fallen into idolatry while he was on the mountain with God, England could certainly do the same.

Problem was, nobody caught the joke. The Dissenters were enraged at being targeted, and many Church of England clergy agreed with him.

Defoe apologized. He even offered to work secretly for the government. But when he realized the punishment was inevitable, he brazened it out. He defended his actions in a poem, "A Hymn to the Pillory," and prepared to face the London mob.

But the crowd had other ideas. Perhaps they enjoyed Defoe taking public officials down a peg. Defoe's three days in the pillory was celebrated. Instead of garbage, Defoe was pelted with flowers. Londoners drank to his health and bought copies of "Hymn" around him.

So if Defoe's pen had sent him to prison, it also set him free. The state recruited Defoe as a propagandist and intelligence agent, and he was even presented to Queen Anne. Defoe's star was rising again, and still to come would be the novels that would secure his fame.

## Stephen Crane Fought the Law (1896)

At twenty-four, newspaper reporter Stephen Crane was riding high. His Civil War novel, *The Red Badge of Courage*, was praised for its accurate depiction of battle, despite the fact that Crane had never seen one. But while doing research for a series of newspaper articles on New York's notorious Tenderloin district, he found himself fighting the city's corrupt police department.

Crane had taken two chorus girls to dinner and was talking about their encounters with the police when they were joined by Dora Clark, a twenty-one-year-old prostitute. Afterward, Crane left Clark and a girl on the sidewalk while he escorted the other girl across the street to a trolley car. He returned to find them being arrested for soliciting by policeman Charles Becker. The chorus girl claimed that Crane was her husband, so she was released. Clark, however, was taken to the police station.

Despite being warned not to interfere, Crane showed up the next day and testified on Clark's behalf. She was released, and his article about the incident won Crane praise for showing the "badge of courage," while making the police look bad.

It might have ended there, except Clark sued Becker for false arrest. Crane agreed to testify again, but this time walked into a trap. The police had searched his apartment and questioned his neighbors. On the stand, Crane was confronted with his opium pipe and evidence that he had lived with a prostitute. Becker was acquitted.

Crane felt humiliated. "My name in New York is synonymous with mud," he told a friend, and quickly left town to cover an uprising in Cuba.

Officer Becker, meanwhile, had one more contribution to make to literature. In 1915, he was convicted of killing gambler Herman Rosenthal and became the first New York City policeman to be executed for murder. In F. Scott Fitzgerald's *Great Gatsby*, mobster Meyer Wolfsheim reminisces with Nick Carraway about drinking at the old Metropole hotel the night Rosy Rosenthal was shot:

> "Then he went out on the sidewalk, and they shot him three times in his full belly and drove away."
>
> "Four of them were electrocuted," I said, remembering.
>
> "Five, with Becker."

## A Twist Ending for O. Henry (1901)

While William Sydney Porter is more commonly known as short-story writer O. Henry, he was known to the state of Ohio as inmate 30664 when he did hard time for embezzlement.

Porter's path to prison began at the First National Bank in Austin, Texas, where he worked as a teller for the owner, who was also his father-in-law. After he quit to pursue his writing career, an audit showed that more than $1,000 had been stolen from his accounts on three occasions. Porter was charged, so he fled to Honduras, leaving behind his family. He had planned for them to join him, but his wife's tuberculosis turned serious. He returned home, surrendered, and was bailed out so he could care for his wife, who died five months later.

A grieving Porter said little at his trial, and he was convicted and given five years. But the evidence against him was shaky. The bank was so carelessly managed that it was common for customers to help themselves to the till and leave a note. There were even suspicions that Porter's father-in-law had taken the money, and Porter was taking the fall. Porter didn't even point out that one of the suspicious withdrawals took place a year after he left.

In prison, he was a model inmate. A licensed pharmacist, he was given the job of night drug clerk and his own room in the hospital wing, where he listened to stories from fellow inmates and worked on his writing. Only his closest friends knew where he was. His nine-year-old daughter, cared for by his wife's parents, was told only that Dad was "away on business."

But in a twist that O. Henry would have appreciated, it was in prison that he found success as a writer. Magazines began publishing his stories, signed with his new moniker: "O. Henry." He never explained to anyone's satisfaction why he chose that name, but one biographer speculated that it was a shortened form of his place where he spent his darkest hours: the OHio penitENtiaRY.

O. Henry managed to keep his criminal past a secret until his death in 1910. Six years later, the *New York Times* revealed the story and that the hero of one of Porter's most famous stories, "A Retrieved Reformation," was based on Jimmie Connors, the prison's day drug clerk and convicted safecracker.

## "Shoot the Bitch and Write a Book" (1951)

The killing of Joan Vollmer is one of the central stories in the history of the Beats and the making of William S. Burroughs as a writer.

Burroughs and Vollmer had been living on a $200-a-month allowance from his parents when they moved to Mexico City to pursue their interests: Burroughs in heroin and hallucinogens and Vollmer in Benzedrine and alcohol.

On a September afternoon, they attended a drinking party. Burroughs took along their four-year-old son and a .38-caliber automatic that he wanted to sell.

During a lull in the conversation, Burroughs took out his gun and told Joan, "It's time for our William Tell act." She stood, turned sideways and placed a glass on her head. He fired, missing the glass, but not her head.

Although given a suspended sentence for criminal negligence, Vollmer's death haunted Burroughs for the rest of his life. He worried that he subconsciously wanted to kill her and believed that he was possessed by an "ugly spirit" that could only be exorcised through writing.

"Shoot the bitch and write a book, that's what I did," he said shortly before his death in 1997.

The result was *Junkie*, his autobiographical account of his drug addiction that was published in 1953. Soon to follow would be *Naked Lunch*, which would make him notorious.

Over time, the story of Vollmer's death has morphed, depending on who tells it. Burroughs would call the "William Tell" story a rumor, forgetting that it was what he told the police (he would also tell them he was displaying the gun and it went off accidentally). The choice of target would change too: anything from a wineglass to a whiskey glass, water glass, champagne glass, apricot, orange, or tin can. Burroughs's son summed up his mother's death in probably the most poetic account: "she placed an apple or an apricot or a grape or myself on her head and challenged my father to shoot."

## Norman Mailer's Song (1981)

For a man who knifed his second wife and sucker punched his friends, Norman Mailer would probably agree that literary talent doesn't necessarily make you a nice guy.

While working on *The Executioner's Song* about convicted killer Gary Gilmore, Mailer received a letter from Jack Henry Abbott. The longtime convict, who had spent much of his time in prison reading leftist philosophy and Karl Marx, offered Mailer his insights into prison life.

Mailer was enchanted with Abbott, his long criminal record, which included robbery and manslaughter, and his criticisms of American society. He seemed the prototype of the existential outlaw hero Mailer praised in essays such as "The White Negro." He got Abbott's prison letters published, rounded up support from his literary friends and celebrities, and promised the parole board that Abbott would work for Mailer if he was released. Over the objections of prison officials, Abbott was paroled.

For a while, Abbott was the golden boy of the New York literary world. The magazines raved. He appeared with Mailer on television and was photographed by Jill Krementz, Kurt Vonnegut's wife.

But Abbott was still a crook with the hair-trigger temper. Told he couldn't use the staff restroom at a small Manhattan café, he stabbed waiter Richard Adan in the chest and left him dying on the street. Instead of finding his Jean Genet or Eldridge Cleaver, outlaws who transformed themselves into artists, Mailer had set loose a psychopath.

At Abbott's murder trial, Mailer doubled down, saying he was "willing to gamble with a portion of society to save this man's talent." This time, his influence wasn't enough to save his existential hero, and Abbott returned to prison.

# Writers' Rap Sheet

Many writers have found themselves on the wrong side of the law:

- In 1661, John Bunyan was given twelve years for preaching without a license. He used his time in prison to write *The Pilgrim's Progress*.
- When King Charles II ascended the throne in 1666, the writings of Cromwell supporter John Milton were burned and an order was issued for his arrest. Only a general amnesty saved him from the death penalty for treason, but he was held in the Tower of London for several months until the king pardoned him.
- The fifteen-year-old future novelist Anne Perry was convicted in 1954 of helping her girlfriend kill her mother in New Zealand. Because of their age, the future mystery writer and her friend spent five years in prison before they were released.
- Playwright Joe Orton and his partner Kenneth Halliwell were given six-month terms in 1962 after they were caught defacing library books, altering their covers, adding funny blurbs, and removing the pictures to decorate their apartment. The vandalized books, now considered literary relics, can be seen today at the Islington Local History Centre.

Mailer had some unusual ideas about the legal system. While running for mayor of New York, he proposed holding jousting contests in Central Park as a way for juvenile delinquents to blow off steam.

# 9

# Unfortunate Encounters

Just because they're writers doesn't
make them brothers (or sisters)
under the skin.

## "Vulgar" Dickens and the "Dreadful Old Ass" Wordsworth (1843)

Great writers do not always make great friends. Consider the case of William Wordsworth and Charles Dickens. In 1843, a mutual friend introduced them to each other. Several days later, the friend asked Wordsworth what he thought of the author of *Oliver Twist* and *The Old Curiosity Shop*:

> After pursing up his lips in a fashion peculiar to him, and swinging one leg over the other, the bare flesh of his ankles appearing over his socks, Wordsworth slowly answered, "Why, I am not much given to turn critic on people I meet. But, as you ask me, I will candidly avow that I thought him a very talkative, vulgar young person—but I dare say he may be very clever. Mind, I don't want to say a word against him, for I have never read a line he has written."

Dickens's opinion of England's poet laureate was blunter: "Like him? Not at all. He is a dreadful Old Ass."

## Dickens Cuts Hans Christian Andersen (1857)

Ben Franklin said that "guests, like fish, begin to smell after three days." Charles Dickens's family would agree after putting up with Danish children's writer Hans Christian Andersen.

Andersen and Dickens admired each other and had exchanged letters and books, so when Andersen visited England, Dickens naturally invited him to stay at his home, Gad's Hill.

Judging from an article he wrote afterward, it seemed like Andersen had a splendid time. He was charmingly welcomed by the family, which consisted of Catherine Dickens, Charles's wife of twenty-one years, and their nine children. He described the cricket games Dickens and the boys played on the lawn, the family's theatricals in their London home, and his moonlit walks with the novelist. He even watched Dickens act in the melodrama *The Frozen Deep* before Queen Victoria.

In one vivid anecdote, when Andersen was depressed over a bad book review, Dickens reassured him with a kiss on the cheek. "They are forgotten in a week," he said, "but your book will live!" He scratched his foot in the sand. "That is criticism." He smoothed it over and added: "Gone!—But that which God has given you, that will remain."

What the article didn't mention was that, although Dickens had urged Andersen to stay for five weeks, the family had tired of his presence. After three weeks, he recorded in his diary that everyone but Dickens was ignoring him. In fact, after Andersen had moved out of the guest bedroom, Dickens stuck a card in the mirror: "Hans Andersen slept in this room for five weeks—which seemed to the family AGES!"

Back home, Andersen wrote to Dickens expressing his gratitude, and Dickens cordially replied. Andersen wrote several more letters and sent his books. But, curiously, Dickens never responded.

What happened? The clue lies in Andersen's article. By the time Dickens read it in 1860, he had separated from his wife and secretly taken up with an actress, Ellen Ternan. He had cut out of his life all his friends who supported Mrs. Dickens, and from Andersen's description of the happy family, he might have concluded that the Dane was among them.

But there might be more. A month after Andersen saw *The Frozen Deep*, Dickens performed the play again in Manchester, only with a crucial addition to the cast: Ellen Ternan. It was their first, fateful meeting.

Seeing his personal life and marriage in print must have scared Dickens. Shortly thereafter, he would keep his secrets by burning nearly all his personal papers and letters.

## Katherine Mansfield Borrows a Book (1916)

You don't make fun of Katherine Mansfield's friends and get away with it.

When she and her friends visited the crowded Café Royal near Piccadilly Circus, they sat at a table next to an Indian man. They ignored him until he was joined by another man and a woman, and from their clipped accents realized that they were university educated.

Their conversation turned to *Armores*, a book of poetry by Mansfield's friend, D. H. Lawrence. The man brought out his copy, and as they read passages from it, they made fun of the poems.

Mansfield and her friends were outraged. They had known Lawrence for years, and Mansfield herself had attended his wedding to

Frieda. She leaned over to the Indians and said sweetly, "Will you let me have that book a moment?"

They did, and she walked out of the restaurant with it. Their polite objections and cries for help fell on deaf ears.

Word quickly spread among London's small intellectual class. The book's owner, Huseyn Shaheed Suhrawardy—later to become prime minister of Pakistan—complained to his friend, Aldous Huxley. Huxley, in turn, asked Ottoline Morrell to find out from Mansfield if it was true.

Mansfield declined to justify her actions to Huxley, saying, "I am afraid I am not young enough to dance to such small piping."

Lawrence, naturally, was told about the battle over the book and proudly immortalized the incident in *Women in Love*.

---

Mansfield's image underwent a change after she died at thirty-four in 1923. Her husband, John Middleton Murry, removed from her published journal her rebelliousness, her malicious asides, and any hint of her extramarital affairs and conflicts in their marriage. Only when the journals were published complete a half century later did the real Mansfield emerge.

---

## Dreiser Throws a Wild Party (1923)

If it takes talent to write a memorable bad book, then it must take an equal amount of skill to host a memorable bad party. On this point, Theodore Dreiser stands alone, for throwing a bash that included H. L. Mencken and F. Scott Fitzgerald and have it be as dull as a wet Sunday afternoon in Bismarck.

It was a cold January night when Carl Van Vechten, Ernest Boyd, Sherwood Anderson, Mencken, and other literary men were invited to Dreiser's Greenwich Village apartment. Many of the men had not been introduced to each other, so for nearly two hours, Dreiser stood in the middle of the room with them sitting on chairs arranged around the walls of the nearly bare living room. One attendee remembered Van Vechten seated in his chair like "an aging madonna lily that had lost its pollen." When Mencken pointed out the lack of alcohol, Dreiser reluctantly broke out the beer, but that and a few of Mencken's jokes failed to break the gloom.

Then the doorbell rang. Fitzgerald had heard about the gathering and, wanting to meet Dreiser, brought along a magnum of champagne and delivered an eloquent speech of homage. Dreiser invited him in, put the bottle in the icebox, and silence again descended on the gathering.

That was the high point of the evening. Dreiser's affair was so memorably bad that accounts of it have shown up in no less than five memoirs.

Dreiser was a contradictory figure. Described as "pudgy, no great talker," he had a habit of going back and forth in a rocking chair while folding a handkerchief into a cube, flinging it out like a flag, and starting the process over again. Yet, he was empathetic with women and able to keep not only a wife but sometimes several girlfriends at the same time.

## Miss Wharton Regrets Meeting
## Mr. Fitzgerald (1925)

It was not the greatest meeting of minds when F. Scott Fitzgerald settled down for Sunday tea with Edith Wharton at her home outside Paris.

The warning signs were there from the first. He had sent her an inscribed copy of *The Great Gatsby*, and she responded politely with an invitation. But the writer in her couldn't resist suggesting that the novel would have been better if the reader knew more about Gatsby's past. And while Fitzgerald admired Wharton enough to send her *Gatsby*, he had also parodied her stories as snooty in a sketch. Just the year before, in fact, he had dismissed her as "having fought the good fight with stone-age weapons."

The meeting at the Pavillon Colombe, Wharton's mansion outside of Paris, played out like a scene from a Jane Austen novel, with the dowager Wharton, waiting for Fitzgerald and his friend Edward Chanler, behind her tea service with her friend, a Cambridge don with the wonderful name of Gaillard Lapsley.

Nervous and fortified by drink, Fitzgerald sallied, "Mrs. Wharton, you have no idea what it means to me to come out here," and was met with a cool nod. The talk turned desultory until Fitzgerald embarked on the story of a honeymooning American couple who arrived in Paris and unwittingly spent their first few days in a brothel. Wharton—either missing the story's point or being ironic about the perception that she was out of touch with real life (opinions differ)—asked what people did in a bordello.

After he left, Wharton commented that there seemed to be something peculiar about the man. Lapsley replied that Fitzgerald was drunk. In her daybook, Wharton noted: "To tea, Teddy Chanler & Scott Fitzgerald, the novelist (horrible)."

They never met again, probably to both their relief.

## Soliciting Eudora Welty (1941)

Among the list of peculiar artistic encounters—such as surrealist Salvador Dalí collaborating with Walt Disney—would have to be added Henry Miller, the iconoclastic author of *Tropic of Cancer*, and the Southern writer Eudora Welty, especially after Miller tried to seduce the proper Southern lady into writing erotica.

Miller was spending the year on the road, examining America for his book *The Air-Conditioned Nightmare*. He had met Welty in Paris, so he arranged to see her for three days in Jackson, Mississippi.

In his letter to her, Miller offered to put her in touch with the "unfailing pornographic market" if she needed the money. Welty shrugged away the offer, but her mortified mother barred Miller from even walking into their house.

Miller's foray into writing blue began in Paris, where he was recruited, along with his lover, Anaïs Nin, and other writers, to crank out stories for a private collector at a buck a page. His suggestion to Welty was nothing more than a friendly way to spread the word of a writing opportunity. Fortunately for literature, Welty didn't need the money.

To ensure respectability, Welty recruited no less than two chaperones to accompany them around town. But she discovered that, instead of the brutish sexual demon found in his books, Miller was "the most boring businessman you can imagine." He was humorless, spoke rarely, and wouldn't take his hat off, even indoors. When he was taken to the same restaurant each night, through a different entrance each time, he expressed amazement that Jackson would have three restaurants.

In Miller's defense, he was probably road weary after six months of travel and grieving from his father's death the month before. He also might have regretted his offer. He found writing dirty stories "devastating" and apologized to Nin for recruiting her, saying, "I don't want to do that work anymore for anything."

## The Wrath of Steinbeck (1944)

John Steinbeck appreciated Ernest Hemingway's writing so much that he wrote a rare fan letter, which sparked a meeting that he would regret.

He had praised Hemingway's short story "The Butterfly and the Tank," so when Papa was passing through New York on his way to cover the D-Day invasion, Steinbeck suggested getting together for a drink.

At the bar, they ran into novelist John O'Hara, who showed Hemingway a walking stick Steinbeck had given him that was made of blackthorn, a particularly tough wood.

"Blackthorn!" Hemingway snorted. "That's no blackthorn." He bet O'Hara $50 that he could break the stick over his head.

Bet made, he balanced the stick on his head, grabbed each end, and snapped it. He threw the pieces into the corner, sneering, "You call that a blackthorn."

Steinbeck seethed. Not only was it a crude, cruel stunt, but the stick had been his grandfather's.

Steinbeck's hatred of Hemingway would last for years. Friends would startle when the usually quiet Steinbeck would break out with "Hemingway . . . that shit!" He would pull *The Sun Also Rises* from the bookshelf and read the dialogue in a flat voice, making it sound horrible. "God damn it," he said, "I don't understand why people think Hemingway can write dialogue."

He got over it eventually. When he heard that Hemingway thought that the end of *The Grapes of Wrath*—when a starving man

# Brief Encounters

- Mark Twain felt Horace Greeley's wrath when, in 1870, the writer burst into the newspaper editor's office looking for a friend. "Well, what in hell do *you* want?" Greeley roared. When Twain stammered, "I was looking for a gentlem—" Greeley shot back, "Don't keep them in stock—clear out!"
- When James Joyce and Marcel Proust met at a supper party in 1922, their talk, according to Joyce, consisted mostly of the word *no*. Proust asked Joyce if he had met some French aristocrat. Joyce said no. When Proust was asked if he had read *Ulysses*, he said no.
- James Joyce was appalled, in turn, when he encountered F. Scott Fitzgerald at a dinner party in 1928. When they were introduced, Fitzgerald kneeled and kissed Joyce's hand. During dinner, Fitzgerald called out embarrassing lines such as "How does it feel to be a great genius, Sir?" and "I am so excited at seeing you, Sir, that I could weep." He rounded out the evening by threatening to leap from the window until Joyce's wife, Nora, said she loved him. "I think he must be mad," Joyce said later. "He'll do himself an injury some day."
- While Sherwood Anderson helped Ernest Hemingway launch his career—urging him to move to Paris and providing him with letters of introduction to the art crowd there—Hemingway returned the favor in 1953 by describing the *Winesburg, Ohio* author as "a slob" and "wet and sort of mushy. . . . From the first time I met him I thought he was a sort of retarded character."

is fed from a dying woman's breasts—was "hardly the solution to our economic problem," Steinbeck wrote, "Mr. Hemingway's analysis is not quite valid but very funny."

---

Like many great writers of the time, Steinbeck drank heavily, and could be a wild man when he had a few drinks under his belt. Once, while working at a fish hatchery, he got drunk on bootleg gin and his foreman found him in his bunk, shooting holes into the ceiling.

## ·10·

# Fight Club

Out of hatred, rivalry, or
orneriness, these writers got along
like bagged weasels.

## Colley Cibber Nukes Alexander Pope (1742)

Poet Alexander Pope was noted for his flame wars with rivals, and one of his chief targets was the popular playwright and poet laureate Colley Cibber. Cibber usually took Pope's ribbing in good humor until he was crowned the King of Dunces in Pope's satirical poem "The Dunciad."

Cibber retaliated by publishing a story describing how he had saved Pope from a potentially fatal dose of the clap which would have deprived the world of his translation of Homer's *Iliad*.

According to Cibber, they had accompanied Lord Warwick to a bawdy house where his lordship proposed pairing the diminutive Pope—who stood under five feet tall—with one of the girls. After waiting several minutes in the next room, Cibber wrote, he "threw open the door upon him, where I found this little hasty hero, like a terrible tomtit, pertly perching upon the mount of love! . . . I fairly laid hold of his heels and actually drew him down safe and sound from his danger.

When Lord Warwick tittered and called Cibber

an hundred silly puppies for my impertinently spoiling the sport . . . I reply'd, pray, my lord, consider what I have done was in regard to the honour of our nation! For would you have had so glorious a work as that of making Homer speak elegant English, cut short by laying up our little gentleman of a malady, which his thin body might never have been cured of? No, my lord! Homer would have been too serious a sacrifice to our evening merriment.

## Flame Wars in the Age of Reason (1766)

When Jean-Jacques Rousseau's attacks on the aristocracy and religion made France and Switzerland too hot for him, David Hume helped find him a refuge in England, despite a warning from Rousseau's enemy Baron D'Holbach that "you're warming a viper in your bosom."

It was a good deed that Hume would quickly regret. Because once settled in England, Rousseau suspected that his letters were being read. He feared that his papers would be seized. He publicly accused Hume of being behind a plot to discredit him.

Hume was shocked. He respected the philosopher and knew that Rousseau had thought highly of him. He wrote Rousseau demanding proof and received a long, blistering letter that was skimpy on the facts. For example, Rousseau wrote he became suspicious of Hume during their journey to England, when he heard Hume mutter in his sleep, *"Je tiens J. J. Rousseau"* (I have J. J. Rousseau).

When Hume published a response to Rousseau's charges, everyone piled on. Anonymous articles appeared in the newspapers, with Rousseau blasted for his lack of gratitude, and Hume roasted for his lack of hospitality.

Was Rousseau right? With Hume's best work behind him, he might have been jealous of Rousseau's popularity. Before extending his offer, he had his friends in France investigate Rousseau's finances to see if he was as poor as he claimed. He may even have contributed to the notorious "King of Prussia" letter, a satire in which the king offered sanctuary to Rousseau, promising, "If you want new misfortunes, I am a king and can make you as miserable as you can wish."

The wildfire of talk eventually burned out. Rousseau returned to France, and Hume was left to reflect on a prescient line from his defense: "Quarrels among men of letters are a scandal to philosophy."

## Byron Beats Up on Keats (1820)

Lord Byron may have considered himself a man of the people, but he was aristocratic to the core when it came to "Jonny Keats," the Cockney son of a stableman.

While living in self-imposed exile in Ravenna, Italy, Byron unburdened his feelings to his publisher, John Murray, after he received a package of the latest books and magazines from him:

> [Instead of sending me Walter Scott's *Monastery*] here are Jonny Keats' piss-a-bed poetry. . . . Pray send me no more poetry but what is rare and decidedly good. There is such a trash of Keats and the like on my tables that I am ashamed to look at them. . . . No more Keats, I entreat, flay him alive; if some of you don't, I must skin him myself. There is no bearing the drivelling idiotism of the manikin.

Meanwhile, the younger Keats admired Byron. He not only imitated his style of dress but even grew a sharp moustache similar to the one Byron wore in Thomas Phillips's portrait.

Byron's private opinion of Keats, however, didn't prevent him from devoting a stanza in "Don Juan" to him, believing that it was a slamming review of his poetry that killed the poet instead of his long-standing tuberculosis:

> *John Keats, who was kill'd off by one critique,*
> *Just as he really promised something great,*
> *If not intelligible, without Greek*
> *Contrived to talk about the Gods of late,*
> *Much as they might have been supposed to speak.*
> *Poor fellow! His was an untoward fate;*
> *'Tis strange the mind, that fiery particle,*
> *Should let itself be snuff'd out by an article.*

**Good thing Keats didn't know what Byron thought of him. Like his father, he had an explosive temper and was noted as a brawler. Someone who knew the young Keats reported "he would fight any one—morning, noon, and night."**

## Poe Charges into the "Longfellow Wars" (1845)

Edgar Allan Poe had a genius for acting as his own worst enemy, and that was especially evident when, with his poem "The Raven" on everyone's lips, he took on America's eminent poet Henry Wadsworth Longfellow.

Poe didn't want to destroy Longfellow, he wanted to wall him up alive as in his "Cask of Amontillado." From the pages of the *Broadway Journal*, which he helped edit, Poe accused Longfellow of stealing from a laundry list of sources: Milton, Tennyson, Scots ballads, even Poe's own unpublished play. When Longfellow declined to respond, Poe wrote a pseudonymous article defending the poet. Then, under his own name, he attacked that article and threw in more plagiarism charges, adding Shakespeare, Pope, Coleridge, and others to the list.

He broadened his attack in another newspaper by reviewing anonymously four volumes of Longfellow's poems. After thanking "Mr. Poe" for exposing "not only a servile imitator, but a most insolent literary thief," he acted as a one-man firing squad, shooting down each poem as "utterly worthless," "mere prose," "exceedingly feeble," "scarcely worth the page it occupies," and "pure inanity."

What lay behind Poe's charges? Mostly jealousy. Longfellow married well, was educated and surrounded by literary supporters, and was able to make a living from his poetry. Poe had none of these advantages. In fact, "The Raven" was extensively pirated and earned him nothing, leaving him "as poor now as ever I was in my life."

By leading the charge in what became known as "The Longfellow Wars," Poe succeeded only in damaging his reputation. But Longfellow forgave him, blaming his sensitive nature "chafed by some indefinite sense of wrong." After Poe died, he even helped the family by buying extra copies of his collected works.

## Mutual Self-Admiration (1883)

*Punch* magazine's publication of a spurious conversation between Oscar Wilde and James McNeill Whistler prompted this exchange of telegrams between the frenemies:

**WILDE:** "Punch too ridiculous. When you and I are together we never talk about anything except ourselves."

**WHISTLER:** "No, no, Oscar, you forget. When you and I are together, we never talk about anything except me."

**WILDE:** "It is true, Jimmy, we were talking about you, but I was thinking of myself."

## Proust Fires First (1897)

Marcel Proust may have been sickly and nervous, but hinting that he was gay brought out the lion in him, and he fought a duel that risked denying the world *Remembrance of Things Past*.

Journalist Jean Lorrain challenged Proust's masculinity when he savaged Proust's first book *Pleasures and Days* in a Paris newspaper. Not only did he slam Anatole France's preface and Madeleine Lemaire's drawings, but hinted that Proust was having an affair with Lemaire's son.

The accusation made Proust nervous because homosexuals at the time risked arrest and blackmail. So to clear his reputation, he challenged Lorrain to a duel.

Ironically, while Proust hid in the closet and dressed like a typical Parisian dandy, Lorrain was a flamboyant homosexual who preferred rouge on his cheeks, henna in his moustache, and bosom-enhancing corsets. His favorite pastime was cruising for sailors, for which he suffered beatings and an occasional drenching in the Seine.

In the days before the fight, Proust's calm behavior impressed his friends. The only thing that concerned him, he said, was that a morning bout would interfere with his habit of sleeping until noon. Once the match was moved to the afternoon, he said, "the duel itself became a matter of no importance."

On a cold and rainy afternoon in the Meudon Forest outside Paris, Proust and Lorrain paced off twenty-five steps and exchanged shots. Proust's bullet hit the ground by Lorrain's foot, Lorrain missed, and the seconds agreed that honor had been satisfied.

Proust called the duel "one of my best memories," a pleasure no doubt enhanced by his later revenge on Lorrain. In *Remembrance*, he based the character of the self-deluded homosexual, Baron de Charlus, on the odious book reviewer.


## Somerset Maugham Slams Hugh Walpole (1930)

Although now largely forgotten, during the 1920s and 1930s, Hugh Walpole was one of England's most popular authors, in large part due to his ability to self-promote and befriend critics and reviewers. His brownnosing was so ubiquitous that Stella Gibbons parodied him in the dedication to her novel *Cold Comfort Farm*, as "Anthony Pookworthy, Esq., A.B.S., L.L.R." (aka Associate Back Scratcher and Licensed Log Roller).

But that was nothing compared to what Somerset Maugham did. One night, while Walpole was undressing for bed, he opened a prepublication copy of Maugham's new novel, *Cakes and Ale* and started reading. Hours later, he noted in his diary, he was still at it, reading with rising horror an "unmistakable portrait of myself. Never slept."

Maugham had created Alroy Kear, a social climber and hypocrite who became successful as much for glad-handing and networking—something not done among Britain's literary class—as for his writing. Kear, Maugham wrote:

> could be counted on to reply for literature at a public dinner and he was invariably on the reception committee formed to

give a proper welcome to a literary celebrity from overseas. No
bazaar lacked an autographed copy of at least one of his books.
He never refused to grant an interview. . . . He generally asked
his interview to luncheon and seldom failed to make a good
impression on him.

At four in the morning, Walpole phoned Maugham's publisher,
demanding that the book be withdrawn. Failing that, he complained to his friends, including Virginia Woolf, who gleefully wrote
that "poor Hugh is most cruelly and maliciously at the same time
unmistakably and amusingly caricatured. . . . He almost wept . . .
in telling us."

Maugham denied that Kear was based on Walpole. Nobody
believed him. Biographers suspect that his spite was piqued after
Walpole gave a lecture on great novelists and left Maugham's name
off his list.

As for Walpole, he tried to fight back by parodying Maugham in
his novels, but he didn't have Maugham's gift for malice. He continued to send Maugham books and friendly notes, but he never
forgave him, noting, "The beggar had drunk my claret."

## Edgar Lee Masters Assassinates Lincoln (1931)

The middle of the Depression was probably not the best time to
savage President Abraham Lincoln, who had led the nation through
an equally dark period, but poet Edgar Lee Masters was a man on
a mission.

His biography, *Lincoln: The Man*, never failed to give its man
an unequal break. Lincoln, Masters wrote, told "sex stories . . . of
the filthy variety." He was cruel to his mother and was mean to his
"unmoral," "shiftless," and "worthless" father. He married for money

and used Christian morality as a cover to drag the nation into the Civil War. Masters concluded that Lincoln was "unmannerly, unkempt, unwashed and untrustworthy."

Some suspected that Masters's target was not Lincoln but his one-time friend Carl Sandburg. The poet's magisterial *Abraham Lincoln: The Prairie Years* had made him wealthy and cemented Lincoln as an American icon. To Masters, whose last successful book was *Spoon River Anthology* in 1915, Sandburg was a "slick Swede" trespassing on Masters's property. Masters's family had lived in Lincoln country for generations, and stories about Honest Abe had passed down through his family. To Masters, Sandburg was "tracking and aping me."

*Lincoln: The Man* set off a firestorm of criticism. Boston booksellers banned it. The *New York Times Book Review* wrote that "Charles Dickens was kinder to Bill Sikes." Even the Klan—no fan of the Great Emancipator—sent Masters a card: "We have our [drawing of an eye] on you!"

As for Sandburg, he restricted his feelings to a private poem, which concluded:

> *Lincoln and Masters one more fable,*
> *One more conglomerate fart*
> *Lost on the anxious rumps of the west wind.*

## Dreiser Slaps Lewis (1931)

It wasn't the best speech Sinclair Lewis made, but it made headlines.

The event was a public dinner thrown for a Russian author. Among the attendees were Theodore Dreiser and a drunken Lewis, who was still stinging over the critical slaps he received the previous year when he won the Nobel Prize for literature (see "Babbitt Does Stockholm," on page 33).

When he was invited to say a few words, Lewis stood and let them have it.

> I feel disinclined to say anything in the presence of the son-of-a-bitch who stole three thousand words from my wife's book and before two sage critics who publicly lamented my receiving the Nobel Prize.

The "son-of-a-bitch" in question was Dreiser. Three years before, Dreiser and Lewis's wife-to-be, journalist Dorothy Thompson, had toured the Soviet Union. When Dreiser's book appeared, Thompson accused him of plagiarizing her newspaper articles.

It was a common slam against Dreiser. He had quoted without credit newspaper articles and court documents in *An American Tragedy*, and a poem of his was considered so close to one by Sherwood Anderson that a New York newspaper columnist ran them side by side to show the similarities.

So after dinner, Dreiser confronted Lewis. "I know you're an ignoramus, but you're crazy," he said and dared Lewis to repeat what he said. He did. Dreiser slapped him and dared him to say it again. Lewis obliged, but before Dreiser could commence a beat-down, his friends hustled him away.

Newspapers nationwide played up the story, but behind the headlines, there might have been more to Lewis's anger than plagiarism. One biographer speculates that, while they toured the Soviet Union, Dreiser might have slept with Lewis's future wife.

**Slapping Lewis made headlines around the world, with most people rooting against the *Main Street* author because, as one newspaper said, he "openly bewailed the intellectual and artistic shortcomings of his own country." One boxing promoter offered to organize a fifteen-round fight, but nothing came of it.**

## Hemingway vs. Stevens (1936)

Sticks and stones may break your bones, but harsh words can lead to a punch in the mouth.

When Ernest Hemingway's sister, Ursula, was introduced to Wallace Stevens at a party in Key West, Florida, the poet from Hartford, Connecticut, told Ursula that her brother was a "sap" and "no man." After the party, a tearful Ursula told Ernest, and he went hunting for the modernist poet.

It was a tough bout to handicap. Stevens was fifty-six to Hemingway's thirty-six, but he was taller, heavier, and had been an amateur boxer. Stevens was also under the influence, but by that time of night, Hemingway usually was, too.

Hemingway caught up to Stevens by the docks and challenged him. Stevens sneered, "You think you're Ernest Hemingway" and threw a punch. Hemingway countered with his fists, and when he was finished, Stevens had not only broken his hand on Hemingway's jaw but also suffered several knockdowns, a black eye, and a bruised face.

Worried about his standing back home, where he was a respected insurance executive, Stevens asked Hemingway not to tell anyone about the fight. While Hemingway agreed, the request rankled him enough to include it in a story he was working on. In "The Short Happy Life of Francis Macomber," after Macomber runs in fright from a lion, he asks the great white hunter, Wilson, not to tell anyone about it.

"He had not expected this," Wilson reflects. "So he's a bloody four-letter man as well as a bloody coward. . . . 'It's supposed to be bad form to ask us not to talk.'"

Stevens probably never learned about this. "About Hemingway," he wrote a friend, "I can say little because I don't read him."

## Donleavy and Behan: Street-Fighting
## Men (1946, 1954)

The friendship between novelist J. P. Donleavy and playwright Brendan Behan was bookended by pubs and street fights, one in Dublin and the other in London.

Donleavy was introduced to Behan in the Davy Byrnes pub that was immortalized in James Joyce's *Ulysses*. Born in the United States to Irish immigrants, Donleavy had moved to Dublin to study at Trinity College. Behan was a hard-drinking poet and Irish Republican Army member who had served time for attempted murder.

As they were chatting, Behan called Donleavy a narrowback, a nickname for Irish emigrants whose backs were not broadened by manual labor. Donleavy took offense and challenged Behan to a fight. Although Behan hadn't meant to insult Donleavy, he also wasn't yellow.

They squared off in the street, but as Donleavy prepared to throw a punch, Behan offered his hand. "Ah, now why should the intelligent likes of us belt each other and fight just to please the bunch of them eegits back inside the pub who wouldn't have the guts to do it themselves."

Donleavy laughed and shook hands. It was the start of a friendship that would see many shared pints, much talk, and Behan's editorial help on Donleavy's classic debut novel, *The Ginger Man*.

The end of their friendship came eight years later when they encountered each other on Fleet Street in London's newspaper district. They spent the day drinking, and when the pubs closed for the afternoon and they were out on the sidewalk, Donleavy mentioned that he had $10 that could be converted into pounds and drunk up.

Behan was enraged that Donleavy didn't mention it when the bars were still open. "You're a no-good, fucking, mean, miserly cunt," he shouted and charged. Donleavy fended him off and was pushed into the middle of Fleet Street. Traffic stopped, horns sounded, and printers and reporters poured out of the buildings and appeared at the windows.

It was a short fight. Behan cursed Donleavy in French, German, and Gaelic. Donleavy feinted and smashed Behan's nose, knocking him down. The police arrived, and the authors were held briefly before being released with a warning. Although Brendan and Donleavy forgave each other, it was the last time they met on a friendly basis.

> **Behan died in 1964 of complications from alcoholism at age forty-one. As his casket passed through the streets of Dublin, mourners opened their bottles of alcohol and poured the first drink onto the ground in his honor.**

## William F. Buckley Loses His Cool (1968)

The politics became personal when liberal Gore Vidal and conservative William F. Buckley Jr. clashed on television while debating events at the 1968 Democratic National Convention in Chicago.

That day, antiwar protesters raised the Vietcong flag outside the convention hall, so Vidal and Buckley were asked if that was the same as raising the Nazi flag during World War II.

Vidal said no, it was a political and free-speech issue. Some people have legitimate reasons to oppose the war.

"You're so naive," Buckley interrupted.

Vidal pushed on. The demonstrators were against the war, and "I assume that the point of American democracy—"

"And some people were pro-Nazi, too."

"—is you can express any point of view you want."

"Some people were pro-Nazi," Buckley said.

"Shut up a minute," Vidal explained.

"No, I won't. Some people were pro-Nazi, and the answer is that they were well treated by people who ostracized them, and I'm for ostracizing people who egg on other people to shoot American Marines and American soldiers. I know you don't care because you don't—"

"As far as I'm concerned," Vidal raised his voice, "the only crypto-Nazi I can think of is yourself. Failing that—"

"Now, listen you queer. Stop calling me a crypto-Nazi or I'll sock you in your goddamn face and you'll stay plastered."

While the moderator tried to restore order, Buckley fired his last shot, telling Vidal to "go back to his pornography and stop making any allusions of Nazism to someone who was infantry in the last war."

Vidal said later the only thing regretted about the encounter was his choice of words. He meant to call Buckley "Fascist-minded."

> The battle between Vidal and Buckley continued a
> year later when *Esquire* magazine invited them to
> write about the encounter. Buckley considered Vidal's
> account so slanderous that he sued him and the
> magazine for libel. The lawsuit was settled with *Esquire*
> agreeing to pay Buckley's legal expenses and to never
> reprint the article.

## Jacqueline Susann Takes on Two Men (1969)

As a bestselling author, Jacqueline Susann was used to being bashed, but John Simon and Truman Capote still managed to shock her.

Round one took place when Susann appeared on David Frost's TV show to promote *Valley of the Dolls*. Frost, writer Nora Ephron, and journalist Jimmy Breslin were on the panel, but at the last minute, Breslin was replaced with someone she had never heard of, the critic John Simon.

She learned quickly who he was when the viperish Simon pointed at her and demanded, "Do you really believe that you are writing art or are you writing trash to make a lot of money?"

Jackie shot back. Imitating his clipped middle-European accent, she wanted to know if he was Josef Goebbels or Wilhelm Goering. "I haff heard of Neil Simon und Simple Simon, but vat Simon are you?"

The interview dissolved into insults. Simon accused her of "smiling through her false teeth." Jackie replied they were capped, but she knew Simon's hair was real "because it's too thin not to be." He shouted he'd "rather see dogs fornicate than read your love story!" This brought a dog trainer running down the aisle shouting that *he* would rather see dogs fornicate than listen to Simon!

That night, as Jackie watched the *Tonight Show*, her husband, Irving, snored beside her, heavily dosed with sleeping pills. Johnny Carson was interviewing Truman Capote, and Jackie herself was about to drift off when she heard her name.

"She looks like a truck driver in drag," Capote lisped in his Southern accent. Jackie tried to shake Irving awake as Capote droned on that she looked like "a born transvestite." She finally poured a pitcher of water on Irving and woke him enough to hear her demand he sue Capote for libel.

Jackie eventually dropped her threat to sue, but she got her revenge on the *Tonight Show* several months later. During the interview, she didn't mention Capote or his remarks at all until Carson finally asked, "What do you think about Truman?"

"Truman?" Jackie paused as if she had to think. "I think history will prove he was one of the best presidents we've had."

## Lights Out for García Márquez (1976)

Gabriel García Márquez is renowned for his works of magical realism, but even he could be tricked with a sucker punch.

At the Mexico City premiere of *Survivor of the Andes*, García Márquez spotted the screenwriter, his longtime friend Mario Vargas Llosa. "Brother!" he shouted and approached Vargas Llosa with his arms open.

But instead of a hug, García Márquez received Vargas Llosa's fist. As his head hit the marble floor, he heard his now-former friend shout, "That's for what you did to Patricia."

The two writers had bonded from the moment they met in 1967, so when Vargas Llosa's marriage hit the rocks, it was natural for his wife to seek advice and support from her husband's best friend.

What transpired between the two is still unknown. Maybe García Márquez advised her to get a divorce. Maybe he consoled her in other ways. Whatever happened, when she returned to Vargas Llosa, he didn't like what she told him.

And when she found out about the fracas at the premiere, she caused one of her own, throwing a vase and several lamps at Vargas Llosa and shouting that he made her look stupid in public.

Another reason behind the punch might be that García Márquez and Vargas Llosa had grown apart. Politically, Vargas Llosa turned conservative, while García Márquez reveled in his friendship with Cuba's Fidel Castro. In literature, García Márquez's *One Hundred Years of Solitude* was recognized as one of the great novels of the twentieth century; Vargas Llosa's latest work was a documentary about rugby players who turned to cannibalism to survive a plane crash in the Andes.

Whatever the reason, the two men have never met since. And nobody's talking.

# The Hellman-McCarthy Steel Cage Match (1980)

An off-the-cuff remark sparked the literary showdown of the century, and battling it out in the ring were two little old literary ladies.

When sixty-seven-year-old Mary McCarthy was asked on Dick Cavett's talk show which writers she thought were overrated, she smacked down seventy-four-year-old Lillian Hellman, calling her "a bad writer, a dishonest writer. . . . I once said in an interview that every word she writes is a lie, including 'and' and 'the.'"

Hellman replied with a defamation suit for more than $2 million.

What was the source of the rancor? It could have been political. Both advocated Communism during the 1930s, but Hellman was a Stalin fan, while McCarthy was on Team Trotsky. It may have been that Hellman once tried to seduce McCarthy's lover. Or it might have been jealousy: McCarthy's career was waning, while Hellman was not just a literary celebrity but a cultural icon. She posed for a Blackglama fur ad that asked "What Becomes a Legend Most?" Jane Fonda portrayed her in *Julia*, her account of how she helped the title character smuggle money through Nazi Germany to the Austrian Resistance before World War II.

So while the lawyers worked, literary New York picked sides. Some who had felt McCarthy's stinging literary criticism supported Hellman, while those who worried about free speech issues backed McCarthy. Pugnacious Norman Mailer played peacemaker, appealing to the women to call the fight a draw. But neither woman would back down.

For McCarthy to win her suit, her lawyers decided to prove Hellman was a liar. They focused on *Julia*. They suspected that her memoir was fictional, but to prove it, they had to identify Julia.

They found Muriel Gardiner. Like Julia, she had studied medicine in Vienna and risked her life helping the anti-Fascists. Unlike Julia (who was murdered in Hellman's book), she was very much alive, and she certainly didn't remember Hellman helping her.

The odds of two female American medical students battling Nazis in Vienna seemed impossibly high even to Hellman's supporters. Hellman stuck to her guns, denying that Gardiner was her Julia but also stubbornly refusing to identify her.

The case dragged on for four years until Hellman died in 1984. McCarthy won, but it was a hollow victory. There was "no satisfaction in having an enemy die," she said. "You have to beat them."

> **McCarthy's sharp tongue got her into frequent trouble. She called a book by Alfred Kazin "permeated with a special kind of oil he produces" and in 1944 joked that she felt sorry for Hitler because he wanted only to be loved.**

## Martin Amis Bites Back (1995)

When the English novelist Martin Amis announced his intention to change agents, the writer Julian Barnes wrote to his longtime friend. He congratulated "Mart" on picking Andrew Wylie and hoped that he would be just as successful as other Wylie clients such as Salman Rushdie, on whose head Iran had placed a price, and Bruce Chatwin, who had died from AIDS.

Julian then signed off his cheery note with two words, as Amis noted: "The words consist of seven letters. Three of them are f's."

Normally, changing agents should not inspire a fuck-off letter, but the agent of twenty-two years that Amis had dropped was Barnes's wife.

The Barnes-Amis implosion thrilled London's literary world, because Amis did more than just drop his friend's wife:

- He picked for his new agent an American who went by the made-for-tabloid moniker of "The Jackal."

- He earned a huge advance—rumored as high as $500,000—for his next novel.

- And he needed the money, it was rumored, so that he could have his teeth fixed.

To British journalists—whose jealousy, envy, and spite are not just characteristics but job requirements—Mart had gone Hollywood, or at least gone New York. He had abandoned the values that

## Acerbic Opinions

No one can beat a good writer when it comes to slanging matches, particularly if the target is another writer.

- William Faulkner on Ernest Hemingway: "He has never been known to use a word that might send a reader to the dictionary."
- Hemingway on Faulkner: "Poor Faulkner. Does he really think big emotions come from big words?"
- Carson McCullers: "I have *more* to say than Hemingway, and God knows, I say it *better* than Faulkner."

ruled Britannica: striving for art instead of lucre, hiring British, and bad teeth.

But lost in the uproar was that Amis wasn't getting his pearlies polished, he was getting them yanked. Heredity and neglect had resulted in the need for a complete rebuild of his choppers. The suffering he underwent, as he described in his memoirs, makes the torture scene in *Marathon Man*—in which Laurence Olivier drills into Dustin Hoffman's teeth without anesthetic—feel like a fluoride rinse. But given the shellacking Amis was getting from the tabloids, with headlines such as "Martin Amis in Greed Storm," it was probably less painful.

· 11 ·

# Ultraviolence

The pen may be mightier than the sword,
but that doesn't mean you should bring a
dictionary to a knife fight.

## Edward Kynaston's Worst Role (1669)

Imitation can cause the severest form of battery.

The Restoration actor Edward Kynaston was considered one of the most beautiful of the boy actors who specialized in female roles. He was also exceptionally vain, particularly of his resemblance to Sir Charles Sedley, the courtier, wit, and playwright whose drunken behavior had once caused a riot on Bow Street (see "Sedley's Obscene Frolic," on page 15).

When Kynaston paraded about London in a copy of Sedley's outfit, the flattery didn't flatter the wit one bit. He hired several thugs to teach the upstart a lesson.

They found Kynaston in St. James Park and asked if he was Sedley; Kynaston preened and said yes. Crying that Sedley had insulted them in a note, they began beating him. Protesting that he wasn't Sedley only made it worse, according to one account: "the more he protested, the more was he chastised, on the ground of his endeavoring to evade punishment by a falsehood."

Kynaston was laid up for a week. King Charles II was furious with his courtier, but Sedley was unmoved. "The fellow has not suffered half so much in body as I have in reputation," he said, "for all the town believes that it was myself that was thus publicly disgraced."

## Dryden Gets Waylaid (1679)

John Dryden, the poet and playwright, was strolling in Covent Garden one evening when, according to a newspaper account, he was set upon "by three persons who called him rogue and son of a whore, knocked him down and dangerously wounded him, but upon his crying out murder, they made their escape."

The fuse behind the attack was an essay circulating in London's coffeehouses. In the Restoration-era's equivalent of the Internet, gentlemen gathered there daily to gossip, conduct business, insult each other, and conduct flame wars in newspapers and pamphlets.

One especially popular pamphlet was "An Essay Upon Satire." Amid its unsigned slurs of King Charles II, his mistresses, and courtiers was a pointed attack on the notorious rake John Wilmot, the second earl of Rochester:

> *False are his words, affected is his wit,*
> *So often does he aim, so seldom hit.*
> *To every face he cringes while he speaks,*
> *But when the back is turn'd, the head he breaks.*
> *Mean in each action, lewd in every limb,*
> *Manners themselves are mischievous in him.*

Rochester suspected that Dryden was behind the attack. He had mentored Dryden, helped punch up some of his plays, and even used his influence to win him the poet laureateship. But when Dryden found another patron who was Rochester's enemy, the two men turned into bitter rivals.

Dryden survived the attack. He offered £50 and a king's pardon for the identity of the thugs, but no one claimed the reward.

---

**We know little of Dryden's private life, but one story handed down has his wife, observing him poring over books in his study, exclaiming: "I wish I were a book, and then I should have more of your company." "Pray, my dear," he replied. "If you do become a book, let it be an almanac, for then I shall change you every year."**

---

## Mary Lamb Had a Little Knife (1796)

Mary Lamb achieved literary fame when she collaborated with her brother, the essayist Charles Lamb, on several children's books, including "Tales from Shakespeare." To see her trading small talk over tea with Samuel Taylor Coleridge and William Hazlitt, it would have been hard to imagine that this was the same woman who plunged a kitchen knife into her mother's chest.

Back then, the family was poor. Mary worked as a seamstress and Charles was a clerk. Her father was senile, and her mother an invalid. In addition to sewing mantuas and dresses, Mary ran the household and got up at all hours to attend to her parents' needs, and suffered from bouts of depression that left her excitable and irritable.

Then one day, the combination of too little sleep, too much work, and too much pressure made her snap. It was lunchtime. Charles was in another part of the house, and Mary was in the kitchen with her apprentice and her mother. She started arguing with her apprentice, then picked up a knife and chased the child around the room. As the girl screamed for help, Mary's mother called on her to stop, and Mary, in a rage, turned on her. Charles raced into the room, but it was too late.

Given the family's history of insanity—Charles had suffered a breakdown the previous year—the court ruled that Mary was a lunatic, and she was sent to the madhouse. A few months later, she was released into her brother's care. They lived together, neither marrying, until Charles's death in 1834.

## Beckett's Close Encounter (1938)

It was a cold January night in Paris and Samuel Beckett was bundled in his heavy overcoat. He and his friends had left the café and were walking home. A pimp named Prudent fell in alongside Beckett and asked for money. Beckett had none. Prudent asked again, and offered the services of his best girl in return for a loan. Beckett refused again and, as they argued, grew irritated and pushed Prudent aside.

Prudent whipped out his knife and plunged it into the writer's chest.

At the hospital, Beckett's bloody clothes were removed, and the doctors found that the thick overcoat had kept the knife from penetrating his heart.

Still, Beckett was seriously wounded, and his friends rallied around him. James Joyce arranged a private room for him. His soon-to-be ex-lover Peggy Guggenheim (see "Make Love the Samuel Beckett Way," on page 172), stopped by. So did Beckett's mother and Suzanne Deschevaux-Dumesnil who would become his lifelong companion.

Beckett recovered and had to go to court to testify against Prudent. On a narrow bench outside the courtroom, he found himself seated next to the pimp. When he asked why he attacked Beckett, Prudent gave a Gallic shrug and said, "I don't know." For this, his fifth conviction, Prudent was given two months.

While critics try to draw a line between Prudent's "I don't know" and the existential themes in Beckett's plays, the playwright thought the incident funny and loved to tell the story. In fact, he admitted that he found the pimp so well mannered and likable that he tried to get the charges dropped.

## Dylan Thomas Under Fire (1945)

It was a bad night at the Black Lion pub in New Quay, South Wales, when British Army Captain William Killick came in and spotted Dylan and Caitlin Thomas. He'd recently come back from spending eighteen months fighting behind the lines in Greece and had learned that his wife, Vera, was using his army pay to support Dylan, who had used his asthma and other stratagems to avoid military service. Worse, the local "curtain-tuggers" were hinting that his Vera had been giving Dylan more than just financial support.

Tempers flew. Insults were traded. A fight ensued. Killick and Thomas were separated, and the couple left, walking back to their rented cottage. Meanwhile, Killick went home and collected his machine gun and a hand grenade.

Dylan and Caitlin were in the living room when they heard the sound of shattering glass in the back of the cottage, followed by the wall exploding with bullets. They flung themselves to the floor, Thomas said, "then Killick came in with the gun . . . he fired the machine gun into the ceiling and said 'you are nothing but a load of egoists.'"

Waving the hand grenade, Killick threatened to finish the job. Fortunately, Thomas's gift for gab was up to the task, and he talked Killick out of pulling the pin.

Killick was tried for attempted murder, but nobody wanted to see him go to prison. The stress he had been under and his war record were taken into account, and he was acquitted. But according to Dylan, he and his wife weren't taking any chances: "Caitlin and I go to bed under the bed."

## Norman the Knife (1960)

When Norman Mailer heard about a friend who had attacked his mistress with a knife, he commented, "God, I wish I had the courage to stab a woman like that. That was a real gutsy act." Years later, he got his chance.

The occasion was a party he had thrown in his New York apartment to launch his campaign for mayor of New York. With the help of his wife, Adele, he planned to win the support of the disenfranchised, and he wanted them to see that he had connections with those who ran the city.

The problem was that the elites didn't want to play, and they ignored his invitation to the party. When Norman's friends such as Allen Ginsberg, George Plimpton, and Norman Podhoretz showed up, they found his apartment jammed with street bums and party crashers from the Bowery.

An upset Mailer drank heavily as the party grew more raucous. He got into fistfights and received a black eye. By the time the last guests left, it was 3:30 a.m., and Norman and Adele began arguing in the kitchen. Perhaps Adele's sharp tongue had set him off; one report said she jeered that Dostoyevsky was a better writer than he.

# Highlight Reel

Norman Mailer was as prolific with his fists as he was with his opinions. Here are some of his classic bouts:

- Jerry Leiber: In 1967, at the popular restaurant Elaine's, Mailer attacked the songwriter from behind and got kicked into a wall, smashing the plaster. Mailer tried to eye gouge Leiber, and a waiter did the same to Mailer. Elaine herself broke up the fight by threatening to bar Leiber if he knocked out Mailer.

- Bruce Jay Friedman: The novelist and screenwriter was on the receiving end of a Mailer headbutt after he messed up Norman's hair at a party in 1968. As Friedman got in his car, Mailer unleashed his fury on the car, hammering it several times. Friedman got out, took a headbutt to the chest, and threw a punch. They were separated again, and Friedman drove off with Mailer again punching the windows.

- Rip Torn: As part of an improvised scene in Mailer's 1970 movie *Maidstone*, Torn nearly brained the director and star with a hammer, wrestled him to the ground, and choked him. Mailer bit off part of Torn's ear and fought back until they were separated by Mailer's fourth wife, Beverly, and his children.

- Gore Vidal I: After Vidal compared Mailer's *Prisoner of Sex* to "three days of menstrual flow" in 1971, Mailer headbutted him in the green room of *The Dick Cavett Show*.

- Gore Vidal II: At a New York party in 1977, Mailer threw a drink and then knocked Vidal to the floor. Vidal got the last word, however: "Words fail Norman Mailer yet again."

Whatever the cause, Norman punctured her chest and back with his two-inch pocketknife, nicking her cardiac sac and nearly killing her.

Adele recovered, decided not to press charges, and received a divorce. Mailer pleaded guilty to third-degree assault and received a suspended sentence. But what concerned him most was not his wife's health or going to jail, but being committed to a mental hospital, because, as he told the judge, "for the rest of my life my work will be considered as the work of a man with a disordered mind."

# Politics and Power

Some writers found that taking sides
made them targets.

## Shelley Shoots at the Devil (1813)

Poet Percy Bysshe Shelley was destined to raise hell. Essayist William Hazlitt wrote that he had "a fire in his eye, a fever in his blood, a maggot in his brain, [and] a hectic flutter in his speech, which mark out the philosophic fanatic." But even Shelley knew his limits.

Two years after he was expelled from Oxford for advocating atheism, he was espousing radical causes in Ireland with his wife, Mary. He distributed pamphlets in Dublin advocating Catholic emancipation, but he found the city's poor—"assuredly the meanest and most miserable of all"—were in no condition for revolution.

Next, the couple tried Wales, where they met a similar reception. Forced to move repeatedly, Shelley continued to agitate, even dropping his messages in bottles and sending them up in small hot-air balloons. But in Tremadoc, Wales, in the isolation of a rural house overlooking a valley, his agitation caused a frightening backlash.

In the middle of the night, Shelley heard a noise. Armed with two pistols and in his nightclothes, he crept through the house and encountered an intruder. Shots were fired, and after a struggle, the man fled. The house quieted down, but later that night, the intruder returned, and a shot pierced Shelley's nightclothes and hit the wainscoting.

The couple fled Wales that day. From the road, Shelley wrote a friend, "I have just escaped an atrocious assassination. Oh, send £20 if you have it! You will perhaps hear of me no more!"

Shelley suspected the attempt was tied to a quarry owner who objected to Shelley's attempt to radicalize his workers. Other times, he claimed it was the devil and even drew a picture of his nemesis.

Or it might have been shepherds. Shelley would take regular walks in the fields, and whenever he encountered a sickly sheep, he would put it out of its misery without asking the owners. Small wonder they'd try to put down the poet.

Whatever its source, the scare worked. While Shelley would continue to agitate for his pet causes, he would limit his efforts to his pen.

## Dostoyevsky's Terrible, Horrible, No-Good, Very Bad Day (1849)

On a freezing December day, several closed carts rolled across the snowy ground at the Semyonovsky Parade Ground in St. Petersburg. The twenty-four prisoners inside were ordered to get out and stand on a platform next to three stakes. They had been given white shirts to wear, a common practice for men about to be executed by firing squad.

Among the shivering men was Fyodor Dostoyevsky. The twenty-seven-year-old former military engineer had enjoyed a brief vogue as a writer, but as his star faded, he joined a circle of intellectuals who discussed socialism, equal rights for women, the monarchy, and other banned ideas.

As they planned to set up an underground printing press to disseminate their ideas, an informer told on them. The year before, revolutions had rocked Europe, and Tzar Nicholas I was determined to protect Russia. So, at four in the morning, the secret police crashed into Dostoyevsky's apartment and arrested him, along with thirty-four others.

After months of questioning, Dostoyevsky confessed, not just to conspiring to publish forbidden Western ideas but to organize a rebellion and free the serfs.

Before the crowd on the parade ground, the charges were read as well as the punishment: "Sentenced to death by firing squad." Dostoyevsky watched in a daze as three men were tied to the stakes, their eyes bound with black cloth, and the soldiers prepared to fire.

Then, the officer stepped forward. He read another proclamation from the tzar that commuted the sentences. Instead of death by lead poisoning, Dostoyevsky was sentenced to four years in a Siberian prison camp, followed by six years of army service in what is now Kazakhstan.

A decade later, Dostoyevsky returned to St. Petersburg a changed man. He found his faith in Siberia and abandoned Western ideas for Russian nationalism, and his writing would extol as virtues humility, submission, and suffering, all of which he experienced as he waited for death.

---

**Dostoyevsky described his time in Siberia as being "shut up in a coffin." Living in the dilapidated barracks, he wrote, meant "in summer, intolerable closeness; in winter, unendurable cold. All the floors were rotten. Filth on the floors an inch thick; one could slip and fall. . . . We were packed like herrings in a barrel. . . . Fleas, lice, and black beetles by the bushel."**

---

## Ida B. Wells Loses Her Seat (1884)

When Rosa Parks challenged segregation in 1955 by refusing to move to the back of the bus, she was following in the steps of a twenty-one-year-old black woman who faced down racial segregation seven decades before.

Ida B. Wells was riding in the ladies' coach on the Chesapeake & Ohio Railroad to her teaching job in Woodstock, Tennessee, when the conductor, following state law, ordered her to move to the colored train car. She refused. The confrontation grew heated. When he tried to drag her away, she chomped down on his hand.

He confronted her again at the next station, with the help of the stationmaster and the baggage man. Wells braced herself in the seat and resisted until she was pulled out of the seat. Wells stormed off the train rather than sit in the segregated car.

Wells wrote a newspaper article about her treatment on the train. She also hired the only black lawyer in Memphis and sued the railroad. When she found out he had been bribed to lose the case, she hired a white lawyer, James Greer, who had been a Union officer during the Civil War. He won the case in the circuit court, and the railroad was ordered to pay $500 in damages.

The Memphis newspaper announced "A Darky Damsel Obtains a Verdict for Damages Against the Chesapeake & Ohio Railroad." But the railroad fought back, secretly offering her several hundred dollars to publicly recant. After she rejected the bribe, the railroad appealed to the Tennessee Supreme Court. In 1887, the court sided against Wells, concluding that she had intended to "harass" the railroad. Worse, it ordered her to pay $200 in court costs.

"O God is there no redress, no peace, no justice in this land for us?" she wrote in her diary. But the court case launched her new career as a journalist, newspaper editor, activist, and writer who crusaded against lynching in the United States.

## When Ezra Met Benito (1933)

Intellectuals and dictators have much in common. Both think they're smarter than the common herd and both cannot tolerate dissent (in the case of writers, from editors, reviewers, and readers). No wonder dictators and artists tend to get along.

Such a meeting of minds occurred when modernist poet Ezra Pound visited Benito Mussolini. Abandoning the artistically provincial United States, Pound had been living in Italy since 1924, and admired Mussolini. He was also a fan of social credit, an economic theory that advocated dispersing power into the hands of consumers and away from governments, banks, and industries, and he hoped to convince Italy's Fascist dictator to adopt it.

At Mussolini's office at the Palazzo Venezia, the poet and Fascist met. Pound gave Mussolini a list of changes to the economy that would be made under the social credit theory, including the banning of all taxes. "Ugh! Have to think about that," Mussolini said.

Then, Pound gave him a copy of his cantos. Flipping through page after page of obscure poetry, Mussolini responded with a noncommittal, "Why, this is amusing," which Pound took as a compliment. A half hour later, the meeting was over, and they parted on good terms.

In the end, Italy would lose the war, Mussolini would be shot, and Pound would be arrested and nearly prosecuted for treason. Instead, he was declared insane and held for several years in a mental hospital. While boarding a ship for Italy in 1958, Pound, for the benefit of the news photographers, threw the Fascist salute, showing that, to the end, he remained Mussolini's biggest fan.

> Pound was so enthralled with "Muss" that he wrote *Jefferson and/or Mussolini,* which compared the dictator to the Sage of Monticello. During the war, Pound made more than a hundred propaganda broadcasts that defended Fascism and attacked the United States.

## Robert Lowell Hunts for Commies (1949)

The writers' colony Yaddo has a reputation as being a supportive place for writers but not for harboring Commies until poet Robert Lowell helped blow the whistle.

The Lowell Affair began when the FBI came calling to inquire about Agnes Smedley, a journalist who had lived in China and written sympathetically about Mao's revolution. For five years, she had lived at Yaddo at the invitation of the colony's longtime executive director, Elizabeth Ames, but hastily left the year before, after an uproar over her political activities.

The agents talked to Ames, Lowell, Flannery O'Conner, and a few other writers, and there the matter ended. But when a U.S. Army report surfaced accusing Smedley of spying for the Soviet Union, Lowell enlisted his future wife, Elizabeth Hardwick; O'Conner; and novelist Edward Maisel to demand that the board fire Ames for being "deeply and mysteriously involved in Mrs. Smedley's political activities."

The army retracted its report, but Lowell pressed his case, and the sixty-four-year-old Ames found herself before Yaddo's board with Lowell acting as prosecutor. There was little evidence to hear, apart from Hardwick and Maisel recounting their interviews with the agents. Ames denied the accusations and chalked them up to "fear and hysteria."

Meanwhile, Lowell's charges became the talk of literary New York. A petition signed by fifty-five writers asked the board to keep Ames, and many more wrote letters in her defense.

By the time the board voted to clear Ames, it became evident that Lowell, not Ames, was the problem. The manic-depressive poet had been having religious visions. He proclaimed O'Connor a saint and embarked on a national tour to proclaim his revelations. But at his first stop in Bloomington, Indiana, Lowell—caught stealing movie tickets and battling police—found himself in a straitjacket and on his way to a padded cell.

> **Madness dogged Robert Lowell throughout his life. No one knew what he would do next: send a telegram to the pope, start conducting at the opera, or sucker punch his wife. On a U.S. goodwill trip to Argentina in 1962, he drank six double martinis for breakfast, and by lunch, he was taking off his clothes and demanding to climb the equestrian statues and sit on the horses.**

# Red Scare Hammers Dashiell Hammett (1951)

Like his fictional detective Sam Spade, Dashiell Hammett didn't complain, didn't explain, and did what he thought was right. His credo was tested when the U.S. government threatened him with prison if he didn't cooperate with the Communist witch hunt.

Hammett had been ordered into a New York courtroom to testify about the whereabouts of four Communist Party members who had jumped bail after their convictions under the Smith Act, which outlawed advocating the overthrow of the U.S. government.

Although he was president of the Civil Rights Congress, which paid their bail, Hammett was leader in name only and probably had nothing to do with their flight. Still, he chose to say nothing. The judge found Hammett guilty of contempt and sentenced him to six months in prison. Soon after his conviction, the IRS filed a lien against him for more than $100,000 in income tax and went after his longtime partner, Lillian Hellman, for $110,000 in taxes on her income as well.

In federal prison in Ashland, Kentucky, Hammett pushed a mop and chatted easily with the other prisoners and the staff. "I don't even seem to get much time to read," he wrote his daughter, "though I've reread *Les Misérables* and liked it better than I remembered, which is also true of some Thomas Hardy I've been rereading . . . One of the nicest features of this place is that chewing tobacco is available."

Hammett served five months and was released on good behavior, but his world was gone. The years of alcohol abuse and heavy smoking had caught up with him, and his health was broken. He had dropped fifteen pounds and was so frail that he had to be helped home. Hellman, meanwhile, had fled the country and returned only to pay the tax bill by selling Hardscrabble Farm, the home they had lived in for twelve years. Hammett had kept true to his beliefs, but he paid a tremendous price.

## CIA Wins Pasternak a Nobel (1958)

When Russian writer Boris Pasternak was informed that he had won the Nobel Prize for literature on the strength of his epic novel *Doctor Zhivago*, he was surprised. He didn't know he was in the running. He would have been shocked if he knew that the Central Intelligence Agency had helped him win it.

Pasternak's story of a doctor-poet and his love, Lara, told against the backdrop of the Russian Revolution, was rejected by a Soviet publishing house in 1955 as "a malicious libel of the USSR" that celebrated the individual over the state. So Pasternak smuggled the manuscript out of the Soviet Union to publisher Giangiacomo Feltrinelli, who had agreed to put out an Italian edition. The KGB pressured Pasternak to get Feltrinelli to withdraw the book. Instead, he played a double game, publicly sending telegrams withdrawing his consent to publish but secretly sending letters encouraging Feltrinelli to push ahead.

Meanwhile, the CIA concluded that Pasternak—who had been nominated for the Nobel Prize for several years for his poetry—could win it with the help of *Zhivago*. But there was a snag: The Swedish Academy would accept the work for consideration only if it was published in its original language.

So when CIA agents learned that Feltrinelli was flying with the *Zhivago* manuscript, they arranged for the plane to make an "emergency" landing in Malta. The manuscript was secretly removed from the publisher's luggage and photographed. Soon, the members of the Swedish Academy received a Russian-language edition of *Doctor Zhivago*.

While Pasternak was pleased with the prize, he was forced to renounce it and was expelled from the Writers' Union. Only the possibility of a public relations disaster kept the Soviets from throwing him into prison. But after Pasternak's death in 1960, they took their revenge out on his mistress, Olga Ivinskaya, who was his inspiration for Lara. For the crime of receiving foreign royalties for *Doctor Zhivago*, she was arrested and sentenced to eight years hard labor.

# I Was Spied On By the FBI

For decades, FBI director J. Edgar Hoover kept track of the comings and goings of many notable writers, but he wasn't a fan. He was looking for Communist leanings, subversive behavior, and un-American beliefs, which to Hoover included promoting racial equality, liberalism, and sympathy for the underdog. Here were a few of his targets:

- Pearl S. Buck: Hoover invited *The Good Earth* author to tour the FBI after she won the Nobel Prize in 1938, but her opposition to discrimination in the armed forces resulted in thirty-five years of surveillance. When she predicted in a pamphlet that after World War II colonialism would have to end, several pages were sent anonymously to the FBI with the words "Sabotage" and "Lies" written in the margins.
- John Steinbeck: Steinbeck's novels urging social and economic justice would put him under scrutiny not only by the FBI, but the U.S. Army and the CIA as well. This led to a paradox during World War II, when he was rejected for a commission in Army Intelligence over doubts about his loyalty, but was accepted as a consultant to the secretary of war. As a war correspondent, he participated in several commando missions (see "Steinbeck Goes Commando," on page 140).
- Lillian Hellman's support for liberal causes resulted in not only an FBI dossier but a baggage search when she flew to Alaska during World War II to visit her lover, Dashiell Hammett, then serving in the U.S. Army. The agent dutifully listed the bag's contents, including that she carried two reference books: H. W. Fowler's *King's English* and *The Little Oxford Dictionary*.

- Bill Mauldin: After World War II, the creator of army soldiers Willie and Joe earned himself an FBI file after he drew editorial cartoons attacking McCarthyism and the FBI's ignoring of lynchings in the South. During his visit to a Texas army base in 1949, he was watched not only by an FBI agent but the army's Counterintelligence Corps.
- Dorothy Parker: The FBI assembled nearly a thousand pages on the Algonquin Round Table wit, bugged fund-raising dinners she attended, and monitored her speeches. She was blacklisted as a screenwriter in 1949 after informers, including gossip columnist Walter Winchell, repeatedly declared that she was a Communist Party member; one neighbor dubbed her "queen of the Communists."

## ·13·

# War

On the battlefield or behind the lines,
these soldiers and civilians revealed
hidden depths.

## Beetle Bailey Coleridge (1793)

Beset by debts and an unhappy love affair, twenty-year-old Samuel Taylor Coleridge fled Cambridge University for the soldiering life. But the future author of "Kubla Khan" and "The Rime of the Ancient Mariner" behaved less like the dashing Harry Flashman and more like Private Bailey.

Swearing his friends to secrecy, he enlisted in the King's Light Dragoons under the name Silas Tomkyn Comberbache. Coleridge proved to be inept at spit-and-polish, although he could confess his shortcomings with eloquence. When a drill sergeant asked, "Whose dirty rifle is this?" Coleridge said, "Is it very, very dirty?" Yes. "Then it must be mine."

He was equally incompetent at riding a horse, falling off one three times in one week. Worse, he developed saddle sores, which he described as "dreadfully troublesome eruptions, which so grimly constellated my Posteriors."

For the sake of his posteriors and the king's horses, Coleridge was moved to guard duty, where he wrote letters for the illiterate soldiers who took care of his gear. According to Thomas de Quincey, his Cambridge education also drew attention from the officers:

> Coleridge, as a private, mounted guard at the door of a room in which his officers happened to give a ball. Two of them had a dispute upon some Greek word or passage when close to Coleridge's station. He interposed his authentic decision of the case. The officers stared as though one of their own horses had sung "Rule Britannia."

Eventually, his family tracked him down, paid his debts, and negotiated his release. They couldn't find a substitute to take his place, but the army had had enough of Coleridge. They declared him insane and threw him out.

Mortified at the attention but grateful to be out of uniform, Coleridge returned to Cambridge. As punishment, he was confined for a month to the college and ordered to translate ninety pages of Greek into English. And for the rest of his life, we can assume, Coleridge never went near a horse if he could help it.

## Winnie-the-Pooh Savages Bertie Wooster (1941)

No good deed goes unpunished, as P. G. Wodehouse learned when a few innocuous radio broadcasts led to accusations of treason and exile from his beloved England.

Wodehouse and his wife were living in France in May 1940 when they were captured during the German invasion. After a stint in an internment camp, the sixty-year-old writer and his wife were moved to a Berlin hotel in 1941, where he agreed to make five radio broadcasts about his internment. Wodehouse had received food parcels and letters from readers in the then-neutral United States, so he thought this would be an easy way of thanking them.

The broadcasts avoided all politics. Instead, Wodehouse talked about his experiences in the camp with typical English understatement and plenty of stiff-upper-lip humor. But to England, broadcasting from the heart of the Third Reich was giving comfort to the enemy. Politicians and newspapers roared their denunciations of Wodehouse, and his books were pulled from the libraries and bookshops.

Among those leading the charge in the press was Winnie-the-Pooh's creator, A. A. Milne. They had been friends but drifted apart, in part because Wodehouse grew more popular while Milne resented being tagged as a children's writer. Further, Milne had been a longtime pacifist, so slagging Wodehouse helped prove his loyalty.

The Wodehouses were released in 1944. While the British intelligence service concluded the broadcasts were not pro-German and unlikely to have helped the enemy, his reputation was still under a shadow. Wodehouse moved to America.

"Nobody could be more anxious than myself . . . that Alan Alexander Milne should trip over a loose bootlace and break his bloody neck," Wodehouse said. But he took his revenge in his characteristically mild fashion. His 1949 golf story introduces a Milne-like writer who uses his son, "Timothy Bobbin," as a source of material. One wonders what Milne thought of the image of him "Up in the nursery, bending over his son Timothy's cot, gathering material for a poem about the unfortunate little rat when asleep."

# Beckett Takes on Hitler (1941)

Although a citizen of neutral Ireland during World War II, Samuel Beckett didn't stand by when Nazi Germany overran France.

At the time, Beckett and his partner, Suzanne Deschevaux-Dumesnil, were living in Paris. Seeing Jewish friends forced to wear the Star of David and Jewish-owned businesses attacked and burned, he knew "you simply couldn't stand by with your arms folded."

He joined the Resistance through Paul Léon, who was his French teacher at Trinity College in Dublin and fellow assistant to James Joyce. Léon hooked him up with a group that was charged with supplying information about the Germans to England.

Beckett would receive information about ship locations, troop movements, and fortifications and type it out on paper that would be reduced to the size of a matchbox. They would be given to a friend, an old lady who looked like a respectable peasant, who would arrange for delivery to England.

But in August 1942, a Catholic priest in the pay of German intelligence betrayed them. Léon was arrested. Beckett and Suzanne warned other members of the cell, packed a few bags, and fled ahead of the soldiers sent to arrest them.

With the help of friends, they sneaked into unoccupied France. They lived out the rest of the war in Roussillon, an isolated village on top of a hill. Beckett helped the farmers in the fields in return for food and worked on his experimental novel *Watt*. They returned to Paris after the liberation and found their apartment nearly as they left it.

For his resistance work, Beckett received the Croix de Guerre and the médaille de la Reconnaissance Française. Characteristically, he told nobody about these decorations—not even his closest friends.

## Steinbeck Goes Commando (1943)

When John Steinbeck covered the Italian campaign in World War II as a war correspondent, his adventures took a turn for Hollywood when he fought on commando missions alongside their leader, the actor Douglas Fairbanks Jr.

The U.S. Navy had formed the secret unit with the help of Fairbanks, who had fought with British commandos. Steinbeck had covered the invasion of Italy with a special-operations unit, which introduced him to Fairbanks.

So nightly, the author of *The Grapes of Wrath* would jump into a flimsy plywood PT boat and risk his life to drop off agents, attack ships, cut communication lines, and conduct hit-and-run raids along the Italian coast.

"As the British say—this is a good show," he wrote home. "I haven't slept in three days more than an hour at a time and I haven't had my clothes off in four days and I smell terrible."

The hairiest mission was when Fairbanks, Steinbeck, and five commandos were sent to capture an island north of Naples that was the site of a major German radar station. The Italians on the island had secretly agreed to surrender, but no one knew how the Germans would react.

The seven men entered the pitch-black harbor in a small whaleboat. As they neared the quay, something roused the Germans, and they fired blindly with machine guns and rifles before pulling back. Fairbanks jumped onto the quay and captured a German officer before he could throw a grenade. Then the seven walked into town and accepted the surrender of the Italians, all 250 of them. Three dozen men from the ship joined them, harassed by snipers, and Fairbanks sent a volunteer into the hills and convinced the ninety Germans that they were outnumbered and to surrender.

The raid, Steinbeck admitted, "scared the shit out of him," and with good reason. According to the laws of war, foreign correspondents were forbidden from carrying weapons or fighting. By taking off his correspondent badge and picking up a Tommy gun before each mission, Steinbeck risked execution.

For his role in the raid, Fairbanks was awarded the Silver Star. Although not eligible, Steinbeck was recommended for one as well.

## Martha Gellhorn Invades Europe (1944)

To cover D-Day, journalist Martha Gellhorn didn't have to fight the Germans, but she went toe-to-toe with both the U.S. military and her husband, Ernest Hemingway.

After three years of marriage, the couple had become estranged. Ernest was drinking more, writing less, and—unlike her—showed no interest in the war. He had seen enough fighting in World War I and the Spanish Civil War. All he wanted to do was get loaded and fish with his Cuban cronies.

But Hemingway's competitive spirit was roused when Gellhorn agreed to cover the invasion of Europe for *Collier's* magazine. Ernest responded by playing dirty. First, he got himself hired by *Collier's*, taking the magazine's sole military accreditation from his wife. Then, he prevented her from crossing the Atlantic with him on a Royal Air Force flight that she had arranged for him.

Gellhorn, in return, talked her way aboard a convoy. For twenty days, the ships zigzagged across the Atlantic, dodging German submarines. They were especially careful because they were ferrying dynamite.

In London, after spending days drinking with his cronies and recuperating from an automobile accident on a blackout-shrouded street, Hemingway was ushered to a destroyer for a front-row seat to the invasion. He made it as far as a landing craft that dropped its soldiers onto Omaha Beach. The next day, he was back in his London hotel, filing his dispatches.

Meanwhile, Gellhorn reached Omaha Beach by a different path. Stowed away on a hospital ship, she reached the coast, where she saw Allied planes roaring overhead and shells bursting on the horizon. As the ship took on the wounded, she worked alongside the doctors and nurses, interpreting in French and German, fetching water, and feeding the injured.

That night, she waded through waist-high water to follow the medics onto the beach. She saw a nightmare scene as red flares lit up the shattered tanks, the blasted pillboxes, and the constant movement of soldiers and supplies across the sand. She took careful notes of the lines of tanks and trucks moving inland, chasing the armies.

In London, she filed two stories for *Collier's* before she was arrested and threatened with deportation by the U.S. Army if she strayed out of bounds again. But she defied authority and slipped away again. For the rest of the war, she traveled one step ahead of the military police, helped along by the soldiers who admired her guts, bravery, and blond good looks.

By the time Berlin fell, she had flown on bombing raids and reported on the liberation of the Dachau concentration camp. She was also divorced from Ernest, who never forgave her for making it ashore ahead of him.

---

**Gellhorn met Hemingway in 1936 in his "odiferous Basque shorts" at Sloppy Joe's bar in Key West. They spent the rest of the day drinking Papa Dobles, consisting of white rum and lime juice swirled in a rusty blender. Soon, they were off to cover the Spanish Civil War and heading for marriage.**

## Marguerite Duras's Dangerous Game (1944)

In occupied France during World War II, Marguerite Duras fought the Nazis alongside the future president of France, seduced a collaborator to save the life of her husband, and lost her heart to a fellow partisan. It reads like *Casablanca*, with spies and Nazis, romance and sacrifice, but with a very French twist.

Marguerite and Robert Antelme had an open marriage, but when she met Dionys Mascolo, she fell so deeply in love that she felt like she was committing adultery. She felt so guilty about her affair that she couldn't tell Robert the truth. So when François Mitterrand asked the Antelmes to join his resistance cell, she brought Mascolo along as well. While Robert helped Mitterrand, Marguerite sheltered cell members at their home and acted as messenger. She also spent as much time as possible with Mascolo, who was also sharing his affections with another woman.

But in June 1944, someone informed on the group. Police raided a meeting and made arrests. Mitterrand escaped, but Robert was caught.

Marguerite visited the police stations and searched the railway stations, looking for news of Robert. While waiting at a prison, she heard the news that the Allies had landed at Normandy. Liberation was coming, but would it be soon enough to save Robert?

Then, Marguerite met Charles Delval, the collaborator who had arrested her husband. He took a liking to Mrs. Antelme. While trying to pump information from him, she agreed to meet him in cafés and, later, in his bed.

Mitterrand and the other members of her cell were worried. Marguerite risked being arrested and tortured. They watched her meetings with Delval and debated killing him.

At a meeting in a café, Delval sprung a trap when he handed

Duras a sheaf of photos. On top was a Resistance leader code-named Morland. Delval explained the deal: Robert Antelme for the identity and location of Morland.

Duras recognized Morland as Mitterrand, but kept a poker face. She denied knowing the man and added, "I don't know how you dare to ask me."

After Paris was liberated, Delval was captured and tried. Duras testified against him, and he was executed in January 1945.

Two months later, Mitterrand was at the newly liberated camp at Dachau, walking among the corpses and near-dead, and heard someone call his name. It was Robert Antelme, weighing eighty-four pounds and suffering from typhus. The fear of spreading disease made it illegal to move the inmates, but Mitterrand pulled some strings, used false papers sent overnight from Paris, and walked him out, disguised in a uniform and passed off as a drunk. His sudden appearance in Paris shocked Marguerite into a screaming fit, but when she recovered, she nursed him back to health.

The perfect Hollywood movie, right? Except that Mascolo stayed with Marguerite and added to his conquests Delval's recently widowed wife. She gave birth to his child in 1946. So did Marguerite the following year, after she divorced Robert.

So very, very French.

Duras's life after the war was equally eventful. She fell passionately in and out of love, drank heavily, quit then resumed drinking, and wrote plenty of novels and screenplays, including the art-house classic *Hiroshima Mon Amour*. She directed numerous avant-garde movies and was still writing when she died in 1996, fifty-one years after the end of the war.

# Alice B. Toklas Springs a War Criminal (1951)

The American expatriate writer Gertrude Stein and her partner, Alice B. Toklas, had every right to feel uneasy when the German Army rolled into Paris in 1940. They were Jewish lesbians whose friendships with "degenerate" artists such as Picasso, Marcel Duchamp, and Marc Chagall could put them on the "must intern" list, especially after Germany declared war on the United States the next year.

Yet they were left alone, thanks to longtime friend Bernard Fay, the historian and Nazi collaborator. Joining the Vichy government headed by Marshal Pétain, Fay organized drives that harassed Jews and Masons, but also protected Stein and Toklas.

"My two friends lived a peaceful life," Fay bragged. "They didn't lack courage, they didn't lack intelligence, they didn't lack a sense of reality, and they didn't lack coal." He was even able to protect their precious art collection.

Naturally, Stein didn't want to admit how they survived the war quite nicely and portrayed herself as bravely facing the danger. They had considered fleeing the Nazis, she wrote, but "it would be awfully uncomfortable and I am fussy about my food." When warned that they could be arrested, she recalled "our large comfortable house with two good servants and a nice big park with trees" and resolved to stay.

After the war, Fay was sentenced to life at hard labor. His propaganda campaign against the Masons had led to the arrest of thousands, many of whom perished in the concentration camps.

Still, Stein and Toklas stood by their man, writing a letter to the court supporting him and sending him candy, food, and vitamins in prison. When, in 1951, Fay escaped from the prison hospital and found refuge in Switzerland, he had Toklas to thank. She had sold some of her precious Picassos to finance the operation.

## Forsyth's Coup (1973)

Writers can get into trouble sticking their noses where other people may not want them to go. Just ask Frederick Forsyth.

In 2009, while researching a novel in Guinea-Bissau, a blast outside his hotel room woke him up. Soldiers angry that the president had killed their general with a bomb the day before had repaid the favor by attacking the presidential villa. From his bedroom window, Forsyth saw them shoot the president as he staggered out of the smoking rubble, then tossed the wounded soon-to-be-ex president into the back of a truck, and he was driven away to a date with their machetes.

But probably the weirdest bit of overreaching came when Forsyth was researching *The Dogs of War*, about a band of mercenaries who attempt to overthrow a corrupt African nation. He'd decided on a country and a strategy and, as part of his research, infiltrated the

---

## Literary Espionage

Not surprisingly, many writers also made good secret agents. After all, both professions require imagination and an ability to lie.

- During World War II, Graham Greene worked for Britain's MI6 alongside Kim Philby, who, it turned out, was also working for the KGB. Even after Philby defected, Greene continued to correspond with him because "he was a good and loyal friend."

- Children's author Arthur Ransome spied in Russia during its revolution on behalf of MI6. He also supported the revolution, writing articles praising it and transporting money to Bolshevik groups abroad.
- Noël Coward's work in Europe before the war put him on the list of British subjects to be executed if the Germans occupied England. When the list was published, Rebecca West, who was also on the list, wittily cabled him: "My dear the people we should have been seen dead with."
- Ernest Hemingway organized a spy ring in Cuba for the FBI during the war to gather information on potential Nazi activities. He also loaded his fishing boat, the *Pilar*, with ammunition and cruised the waters looking for enemy submarines. The plan was to lure the sub to the surface. When the Germans would open the hatch, Hemingway and his pals would ambush them with machine guns and hand grenades. However, no subs took the bait.
- Ian Fleming based his James Bond stories in part on his work in naval intelligence during World War II. To help crack the German's Enigma code, Fleming proposed crashing a German bomber in the English Channel during an air raid with a British crew aboard disguised as Germans and capturing one of their rescue boats with its Enigma paperwork. The plan for "Operation Ruthless" was approved and Fleming assigned himself to the crew. The plan was abandoned only because of a lack of opportunity.

world of black market weaponry. Using a South African name, he came into contact with mercenaries and told them his "plan." They liked his idea so much that they adopted it and targeted tiny Equatorial Guinea.

"I took part in the plot in as much as I was chewing the fat and shooting the breeze with the others involved," Forsyth said. "But as far as I was concerned any money I gave was for information and I pulled out before the plan was put into practice."

Forsyth abandoned the group after one of the arms dealers saw a picture of him in a Hamburg bookstore window, promoting his *Day of the Jackal*. His cover blown, Forsyth grabbed his passport and fled town on the next train.

As for the mercenaries, they got as far as the Canary Islands before an anonymous tip to the British embassy in Madrid led to their arrest by Spanish police. Good thing, too, Forsyth said, "they would have been slaughtered."

> In a real-life sequel to *Dogs of War*, British mercenary Simon Mann was arrested in 2004 with sixty-nine others in Zimbabwe when their Boeing 727 landed at Harare's airport, where it was to be loaded with weapons and equipment for a coup against Equatorial Guinea.

## · PART THREE ·

# Everything Else

# Bad Craziness

Psycho, schitzo, or just a little nutty: The
squirrels were calling their names.

## Richard Sheridan's Poisonous Pen (1805)

Apart from his wife, for whom he risked his life to win (see "Richard
Sheridan Plots an Elopement," on page 165), the other great love of
Richard Sheridan's life was Harriet Duncannon. Beautiful, witty,
and intelligent, she also proved to be his equal as a poet.

They had been lovers, but she broke off relations when the married Sheridan's political enemies threatened to expose them. Sheridan, however, refused to take no for an answer. He would appear
uninvited at her house and use his considerable wit to try and win
her back. Though Harriet was charmed, she firmly said no.

The years passed. Sheridan's political influence ebbed, his wife
died in childbirth, and the couple's infant daughter followed shortly
thereafter. The bereft Sheridan fell apart, physically and mentally.

Then, on New Year's Day, Harriet's daughter, Caroline—later she
would become notorious as Caroline Lamb (see "The Lamb Became
a Tiger," on page 189)—received a letter filled "with every gross,

disgusting indecency that the most depraved imagination could suggest." Two days later, Harriet received a similar letter. More nasty notes followed, some containing pornographic prints. London's newspapers began receiving unsigned articles containing scurrilous gossip about Harriet, her husband, lover, and friends.

Harriet saw Sheridan's hand behind the letters. But instead of confronting him, she published in a London newspaper a poem, chiding the author of the letters:

> Shame to the pen whose coward poisons flow
> In secret streams with baneful malice fraught
> That emulates th' assassins Midnight blow
> By hate directed and vengeance wrought.
> Yet generous Minds the name will ne'er impart,
> But leave the dastard miscreant to feel
> The Conscious pangs of a corrupted heart.

Sheridan took the hint. The letters stopped.

## Shelley Freaks Out (1816)

While summering at a villa in Switzerland, Percy Bysshe Shelley, his wife, Mary; Lord Byron; and other guests whiled away their evenings reading to each other. One night, Byron chose Samuel Taylor Coleridge's "Christabel," an erotically charged poem that in our day would have begun "Dear Penthouse Letters, I never thought this would happen to me, but—"

As the fire crackled, Byron recited the story of Christabel, who wanders the woods at night near her father's castle and encounters the beautiful Geraldine. She tells Christabel that she had been kidnapped and abandoned by five men, so like a good girl, Christabel takes Geraldine back to the castle, where she assures her they'll be quite alone:

> Sir Leoline [her father] is weak in health,
> And may not well awakened be,
> But we will move as if in stealth;
> And I beseech your courtesy,
> This night, to share your couch with me.

Imagine the scene in the firelit room, late at night, with a drink or two in you, listening to the notorious Lord Byron reading this. The atmosphere grows heated until Geraldine

> . . . unbound
> The cincture from beneath her breast:
> Her silken robe, and inner vest,
> Dropt to her feet, and full in view,
> Behold! her bosom and half her side—
> [Are lean and old and foul of hue]
> A sight to dream of, not to tell!
> O shield her! Shield sweet Christabel!

"Silence ensued," an eyewitness wrote, "and Shelley, suddenly shrieking and putting his hands to his head, ran out of the room with a candle. Threw water on his face, and after gave him ether. [He explained] he was looking at Mrs. Shelley, and suddenly thought of a woman he had heard of who had eyes instead of nipples, which, taking hold of his mind, horrified him."

Eyes instead of nipples? I don't think even *Penthouse* covered that kink.

Shelley also suffered from delusions that his father was plotting to arrest him. They had parted over Shelley's atheism and his abandoning of his wife for Mary Godwin. It didn't help that, at one of their last meetings, while the old man was weeping and lecturing his son, Shelley imagined his father as Jehovah with a handkerchief and laughed so hard he fell out of his chair.

## Sherwood Anderson Bugs Out (1912)

On the surface, Sherwood Anderson looked every inch the prosperous middle-class businessman of Elyria, Ohio. The owner of the Anderson Manufacturing Co. was a member of the Elks Lodge and played golf at the country club, while his wife took care of their children and attended meetings of the local literary society.

But the man who dreamed of becoming rich and moving to a country estate had a dreadful secret. At night, away from his family, he wrote stories "more or less in secret, as one might indulge in some forbidden vice."

Anderson had discovered that business bored him. His life bored him. The former ad copy writer in Chicago had climbed the ladder of success and found "I was telling people the same kind of lies I had lied before."

Then he couldn't take it anymore. While dictating a letter to his secretary, he paused, and then said, "My feet are cold and wet. I have been walking too long on the bed of a river."

So he headed for dry land, specifically to Cleveland, forty miles away, where he was found, four days later, his face haggard and unshaven, sitting at a drugstore counter.

The newspapers said that he had suffered from severe mental strain from overwork. While he claimed amnesia, he later admitted that some of it was faked: "If men thought me a little insane they would forgive me if I lit out."

He returned to Elyria, but not for long. He left his family and moved back to Chicago, where he resumed his job as a copy writer for an ad agency and the literary career that he would launch two years later.

## The "Monster" William Golding (1930)

If you want to know where William Golding received his insights to depict society degenerating into monsters in *Lord of the Flies*, he only had to look into the mirror.

The self-described "monster in deed, word and thought" saw the world in terms that would have made Samuel Beckett seem like Mister Rogers. To him, man was "this monstrous creature, this biological irrelevance" and life "one long nightmare." If he had been born in Hitler's Germany, he often said, he would have been a Nazi.

Golding was also equally dismissive about women early in life, after a botched seduction turned into attempted rape of a fifteen-year-old girl while he was an Oxford undergraduate.

He had known Dora since she was thirteen, by which time, he wrote in a memoir, he imagined her "beginning to burn." By fourteen, he thought she was "already sexy as an ape." No wonder, when he was visiting home from Oxford, while walking with her, he "felt sure she wanted heavy sex" and tried to seduce her. Soon, they were wrestling on the ground, and Golding discovered he "had made such a bad hand at rape." The encounter ended with her fleeing and the future Nobel Prize winner shouting "I'm not going to hurt you."

But Dora was not finished with Golding. A year later, she enticed him to have sex near a school's playing field. What she didn't tell him was that his brother would also be there having sex with his girlfriend, and that Golding's father, at Dora's suggestion, would spot them in flagrante through binoculars.

As a schoolteacher, Golding admitted manipulating the boys into attacking each other on a field trip to a Neolithic enclosure to observe the result. "I gave them more [liberty] and my eyes came out like organ stops as I watched what was happening."

The result, as we know, is *Lord of the Flies*.

## Roethke's Walk in the Woods (1935)

On November mornings, professors are normally found in classrooms lecturing, not looking hungover and babbling to the dean about cutting his 8 a.m. class to see what the students would do.

But that's what the dean at Michigan State University was faced with when professor Theodore Roethke appeared in his office. Soaked, shivering, and shoeless, he looked like he had spent the night in the woods, which he had. The alarmed dean called an ambulance, and the poet was hauled off to the hospital where he was diagnosed with delirium tremens.

It was a shocking comedown for the newly hired teacher of freshman English. He had come highly recommended by his Harvard professors, and he was a great teacher, encouraging his students to use poetry to investigate their inner selves.

But Roethke quickly became known for his odd behavior. He startled one class by leaping atop his desk and pretending to mow them down with a machine gun. To teach observation, he climbed onto the outside ledge and worked his way around the room, making faces in the windows. Away from class, Roethke drank copious amounts of whisky and beer, and ate aspirin by the handful.

His walk in the woods might have been the result of a nervous breakdown, brought on by too much alcohol. But one of Roethke's poems hints that he might have been searching for the secret of Nijinsky. The Russian dancer and choreographer had written about his desire to learn wisdom through following his "trance of feelings" no matter where it led, and he described a similar stroll through the forest.

Only Roethke knew if he found wisdom in the woods. Certainly the dean had; he told his wayward professor that "budget changes" meant his services were no longer needed at Michigan State University.

## Patricia Highsmith the Stalker (1948)

The woman was tall and blond, the way Patricia Highsmith liked them, and their brief encounter would inspire a landmark lesbian novel.

Kathleen Senn was at Bloomingdale's to buy a doll for her daughter, and the twenty-eight-year-old Highsmith—a few years away from writing *Strangers on a Train* and her novels about the murderous Tom Ripley—was clerking in the toy department and writing comic books. She made the sale and arranged to have the doll delivered to Senn's home in New Jersey.

That was the only time they met, but it inspired Highsmith—a brittle, closeted lesbian—to begin *The Price of Salt*. The novel about the relationship between a department store clerk and a divorcee would sell over a million paperback copies and was unique in lesbian lit for its happy ending.

But after finishing the novel, Kathleen was still on Highsmith's mind. Twice, she took the train to New Jersey, where she wandered the streets near Senn's house. A brief glimpse of Kathleen as she drove by inspired an unusual reaction in Highsmith: She wanted to murder her. As she explained in her diary:

> Murder is a kind of making love, a kind of possessing. (Is it not, too, a way of gaining complete and passionate attention, for a moment, from the object of one's attentions?)

Senn, who beneath her cool exterior was a mentally depressed alcoholic, never knew of her role as Highsmith's muse. Shortly before the novel was published, she stepped into her garage, turned on the car's engine, and killed herself.

---

**Highsmith also stalked Greta Garbo on the streets of New York, although from a respectful distance. When she almost collided with the retired actress on a street corner, Highsmith recalled the encounter made her day.**

---

## Janet Frame's Close Call (1952)

Literature gave purpose and meaning to New Zealand author Janet Frame's life. It also saved her mind.

Mistakenly diagnosed with schizophrenia, Frame had been in and out of mental institutions for years, where she had been subjected to shock treatments using electricity and insulin injections.

But Frame kept writing, and four years into her latest stay at Seacliff Mental Asylum, her first book of short stories, *The Lagoon and Other Stories*, had been published. Her pleasure in its publication was cut short when she read a newspaper review that trashed the book as imitative, pointless, and sentimental. Her humiliation so overshadowed other, more favorable, reviews, that she would remember this one, word for word, for the rest of her life.

Meanwhile, believing her illness couldn't be cured, her doctor decided to perform a prefrontal lobotomy, which would sever the front part of the brain from the cerebral cortex. Although reassured that she would be "out of hospital in no time," Frame felt a "swamping wave of horror" at the possibility of having her mind wiped.

Then her fortune changed. Only days before the surgery, New Zealand's chapter of PEN awarded her its literary award for *The Lagoon and Other Stories*. The hospital superintendent informed her of the award and canceled the operation. "I've decided that you should stay as you are," he told her. "I don't want you changed."

Frame understood how close she came to disaster. In the same hospital was the daughter of her college lecturer who was committed in the belief that her asthma was psychosomatic. She received the lobotomy scheduled for Frame. Instead of curing her asthma, it made it worse, and she was in and out of psychiatric hospitals for the rest of her life.

"The legacy of her dehumanising change remains . . . with all who knew her," Frame said. "I have it with me always."

## Anne Sexton Hits the Road (1966)

When high school teacher Robert Clawson picked up Anne Sexton for a weeklong conference in the East Hamptons, he wondered why her family told her to "take care of Mom."

He got the first hint when Mom pulled out a six-pack of beer and popped the top, because in addition to being a brilliant confessional poet, Sexton was an alcoholic and mentally unstable.

At first, the trip went fine. He drove them to New London,

Connecticut, where he pulled his convertible onto the ferry for the trip across Long Island Sound.

That night, when he met her at the car after dinner, Robert found Anne in a trance, looking at the trees and murmuring. He broke the trance with a kiss. Anne asked him to drive to the beach, where they walked on the sand and watched the waves roll in. "You know what the waves say?" she said. "They say I am, I am." They became lovers.

The conference ended on an inauspicious note. A misunderstanding arose when Clawson thought Anne had spent the night with another man. When he confessed his suspicions, she showed him a sheaf of poems and said she had been writing them for him. (She hadn't; they were meant for her therapist, with whom she was carrying on an affair.) She begged him to run away with her to Mexico. When he pointed out they had no money, she contemptuously burned a twenty-dollar bill at the table.

Her behavior turned bizarre on the ride home. She jumped out of the car at a gas station and fled into the fields. On the ferry, Clawson had to keep her from jumping into the water, to the point of following her into the bathroom to ensure she didn't climb out of the window.

By the time they returned home, Clawson no doubt decided that mothering Anne was best left to her family.

---

**When Sexton told her psychiatrist that she would make a good prostitute—and had been practicing on men she picked up in parking lots—he suggested writing poems instead. A televised lecture on the sonnet form taught her the basics, and by the end of the year, she had written sixty. Their quality convinced a Harvard professor to enroll her in a poetry class.**

## The Fish That Ate Philip K. Dick (1974)

On paper, science-fiction writer Philip K. Dick explored worlds where the line blurred between fantasy and reality. Not surprising, the same thing happened to him in real life.

## Literary Hangouts: Bellevue Hospital

There should be a plaque outside New York's Bellevue Psychiatric Hospital, where some of America's great writers stayed.

- Playwright Eugene O'Neill stayed there in 1912 after a suicide attempt over the breakup of his first marriage.
- Both William Burroughs and his wife, Joan Vollmer, were residents on separate occasions before they ended up in Mexico, where he killed her (see "Shoot the Bitch and Write a Book," on page 83). Burroughs was sent there when, obsessed with a young man, he severed a fingertip with poultry shears.
- Allen Ginsberg was a guest in 1949 after pleading insanity for allowing a junkie to store stolen goods in his apartment. It was there that he met Carl Solomon, to whom he dedicated *Howl* and immortalized as the man who "talked continuously seventy hours from park to pad to bar to Bellevue to museum to the Brooklyn Bridge."
- Norman Mailer stayed there in 1960 after stabbing his wife after a party (see "Norman the Knife," on page 122).
- Poet Delmore Schwartz came to stay in 1957 after attacking a man who he thought was sleeping with his wife.

In great pain after his wisdom teeth were extracted, Dick was awaiting a delivery of pain medication to his home when the doorbell rang. When he answered the door, he was dazzled by the sunlight reflecting off the delivery girl's Christian fish necklace. For an instant, he thought he was living in the Roman Empire after Jesus Christ was crucified.

Dick went down the rabbit hole. For two years, he experienced intense visions that would come to others only with the help of powerful hallucinogens. He would fall into a trance and mutter in Greek. A pinkish light would strike him, and he would be overwhelmed with information from an unknown source.

For one month, Dick thought he was living in Roman times. He lost the ability to drive and saw police officers as Roman soldiers hunting for Christians. In another incident, he believed himself possessed by Elijah's spirit.

Then one day, while listening to "Strawberry Fields Forever," Dick fell into a trance, and the lyrics warned him that his infant son was suffering from a potentially fatal inguinal hernia. He ordered his wife to take their child to the doctor, where the diagnosis was confirmed.

Dick would spend the rest of his life filling notebooks with his theories behind his visions, which he also used in his novels *Valis* and *Radio Free Albemuth*. While his experiences suggest schizophrenia helped by longtime amphetamine abuse, the depth and consistency of his visions do not. There's no doubt that *something* happened to Philip K. Dick, but the question remains: what?

# ·15·

# The Lovers

Love is like a sled heading for a cliff, but
they went along for the ride anyway.

## Donne Undone (1602)

If you're going to marry into the boss's family, as John Donne should
have learned, the worst time to tell your father-in-law is three weeks
after the wedding.

After serving with the earl of Essex on several military cam-
paigns against the Spanish, the twenty-five-year-old future poet
became chief secretary to Sir Thomas Egerton, who was the Lord
Keeper of the Great Seal. As a perk of the job, he stayed in Egerton's
home near the palace at Whitehall, where he met his boss's niece,
Anne More.

Love blossomed and they were married. Donne wrote to his
father-in-law, and after confessing that "about three weeks before
Christmas we married," Donne had the audacity to ask Dad to deal
with it "as the persuasions of nature, reason, wisdom, and Christian-
ity shall inform you."

More's Christian response was to get Donne fired and clapped
into prison.

Donne was not high-born enough for the Tower of London—which was probably fortunate, since Anne's father was lieutenant of the Tower—so he was sent to Fleet Prison instead, along with the priest who had married them.

Eventually, his father-in-law reconciled with John and Anne, but seven years passed until John received her dowry. But for a while, as Donne wrote in a letter to his wife, they were "John Donne, Anne Donne, Un-done."

## Shakespeare's History Lesson (1603)

William Shakespeare left little behind apart from his immortal plays and sonnets, but one amorous adventure was so notorious that it became part of London gossip.

John Manningham, a barrister at the Middle Temple, preserved in his diary entry for March 13, 1603, an anecdote that showed Will as something of a dog around the ladies. When Richard Burbidge was playing the lead in Shakespeare's *Richard III*, he arranged an assignation with a lady for after the performance. Shakespeare heard about it, got there first, and seduced her. When Burbidge arrived and sent word up that her Richard III had arrived, Shakespeare sent a message back that William the Conqueror came first.

> Wherever Shakespeare found love, it certainly wasn't with his wife, Anne. At his death, he left her only "my second best bed with the furniture." While some biographers have tried to put a positive spin on it, it should be noted that in his first draft of the will, he didn't mention his wife at all.

# Richard Sheridan Plots an Elopement (1771)

The way playwright Richard Sheridan eloped with his wife could have supplied the plot for a romance novel.

The nineteen-year-old future playwright and politician was living in Bath with his father when he met Elizabeth Linley. The seventeen-year-old was a talented singer and precocious beauty who didn't lack for admirers, including Sheridan.

Another admirer was Thomas Mathews, a married nobleman who tried to seduce her. When she rejected him, he threatened to blacken her reputation. Fearing that telling her father would cause a duel, she decided to flee for a French convent and needed someone to help her.

Enter Sheridan. Although only a teenager, he called in some favors and improvised a daring plan. The couple fled Bath in the middle of the night for Dover, where they boarded a boat for France. By the time they reached the convent, he had confessed his love for her, and they were secretly married. She was still at the convent when her father tracked them down and escorted them back to England.

At home, further trouble awaited. Their union in a Catholic church was not recognized in England, and both fathers forbade a second marriage. Worse, Sheridan's elopement and Mathews's bullying was the talk of Bath. To save his reputation, Mathews branded Sheridan a liar and a scoundrel. The result was a duel in a London tavern, in which Sheridan won and Mathews was forced to apologize.

Back in Bath, the despicable Mathews recanted his apology and forced a second duel. This time, both men spent the night before drinking, resulting in a wild fight at dawn in a field. The enemies grappled until they broke their swords and flung each other to the ground. Mathews ended up on top, jabbing viciously at Sheridan's neck and face with six inches of broken blade. Both were wounded in the stomach, but Sheridan was clearly getting the worst of it. Their seconds shouted at him to give up, but Sheridan, maddened by pain and pride, screamed, "No, by God, I won't!" Mathews stabbed him in the neck again, and only then did their friends rush in to prevent a murder.

Sheridan suffered five flesh wounds but survived. Even better, eighteen months later, he earned his happy ending by legally marrying Eliza.

## Rabbie Burns Stands for Fornication (1786)

The poet Robert Burns must have had his fingers crossed in his pew at the Scottish Presbyterian church in Mauchline when he stood alongside Jean Armour, his pregnant lover, confessed the sin of fornication before marriage, and sincerely repented.

At age twenty-seven, "Rabbie" Burns had a reputation as a rake. He was handsome and witty, a poet, and a fiddle player. His education as the son of a tenant farmer was erratic, but he absorbed the Scottish oral tradition, read whatever he could get his hands on, and wrote verses, which he used to seduce girls. He had already begot one bastard on his mother's servant, and now he had seduced Jean, a master stonemason's daughter.

But Jean was different from the other girls. Described as "a very comely woman with plain sound sense and very good manners," Robert agreed to marry her, but Jean's father rejected Rabbie and made Jean confess to the church authorities.

On the rebound, Burns seduced another woman, Mary Campbell, and possibly got her pregnant as well. With Jean out of the picture, he decided to take Mary to Jamaica, but to help support his growing family, he compiled his works and published *Poems, Chiefly in the Scottish Dialect.*

Then fate took a hand. *Poems* was a success, and Burns was lionized. In September, Jean gave birth to twins. In October, Mary died, possibly from a premature childbirth. With Jean's father softening toward the successful poet, Robert returned to Mauchline, found Jean pregnant again, and proposed to return to her under one condition: She was not to claim him as a husband. When she agreed, he thanked her in his usual way: "I took the opportunity of some dry horse litter and gave her such a thundering scalade that electrified the very marrow of her bones."

Eventually, they did marry, and despite his affairs, they stayed together for the rest of his life. Jean supported him, bore his children, tolerated his affairs, and even took in one of his bastard daughters, commenting only that "Our Robbie should have had twa [two] wives."

---

Burns's earlier liaison with a family servant possibly resulted in a similar punishment before the church authorities. The records have vanished, but Burns wrote a poem that hinted at it:

> *Before the Congregation wide*
> *I pass'd the muster fairly,*
> *My handsome Betsey by my side,*
> *We gat our ditty rarely;*
> *But my downcast eye by chance did spy*
> *What made my lips to water,*
> *Those limbs so clean where I, between,*
> *Commenc'd a Fornicator.*

## Oscar Wilde Almost Saves Himself (1894)

At the breakfast table at a seaside hotel in Brighton, Oscar Wilde opened the newspaper and sealed his fate.

He was at peace on that October morning. He had resolved to break with his beloved Bosie, aka Lord Alfred Douglas, a slender Oxford student with pale skin and blond hair. Douglas was charming and beautiful, but a spendthrift and spoiled, and his father, John Sholto Douglas, the marquis of Queensberry, had been raising hell over their relationship.

Wilde's summer had begun with his family at Worthing. It was a happy time, with Wilde writing *The Importance of Being Earnest*, enjoying the company of his wife, Constance, and playing with his boys on the beach.

The good times ended in October when Bosie joined them. Relations between him and Constance were tense, and she left for London with the boys.

Wilde and Bosie took rooms at a Brighton hotel, where Bosie caught influenza. He spent a week in bed, with Wilde devotedly nursing him.

Then Wilde fell ill, and Bosie was revolted. He raged when Wilde wanted to stay in bed and abandoned him to suffer, returning only to demand money. When he moved out, he stuck Wilde with the bill.

Enough was enough. "Ill as I was," Wilde recalled, "I felt at ease. The fact that the separation was irrevocable gave me peace."

But over breakfast, Wilde read that Bosie's eldest brother, Francis, had been found dead in a ditch with his shotgun beside him. Wilde's heart melted. Francis's death was, Wilde wrote, "the first noble sorrow" of Bosie's life, and he rushed to his lover's side, forgiving all.

But to Queensberry, his heir's death cemented his decision to destroy Wilde. Francis had been having an affair with the prime minister, Lord Rosebery. Queensberry had evidence and threatened Rosebery with exposure. The death was ruled an accident, but there was no doubt to many that Francis had killed himself to protect his lover.

Queensberry became Wilde's nemesis and eventually succeeded. For loving Bosie, Wilde would experience disgrace, prison, and exile to France, where he died six years later.

## Somerset Maugham: No Good Deed (1917)

When the English writer Somerset Maugham married Syrie Wellcome, one wag described the odd coupling as "the only time in his life that Willie behaved like a gentleman; the result was fatal."

When Maugham fell for Syrie, she was at the apex of a triangle, married to Henry Wellcome and having an affair with Malcolm Selfridge, the tycoon founder of the Selfridge department store chain. The bisexual Maugham was so enthralled with her that he agreed to father a child with her. After all, she told him, her husband would not mind, and she had broken with Selfridge.

But Syrie had lied on both counts. When Wellcome found out about the affair, he sued for divorce, naming Maugham as the corespondent. Rather than abandon his newborn daughter, Maugham agreed to do the right thing and marry Syrie. The justice of the peace in Jersey City, New Jersey, performed the ceremony in between the sentencing of two drunks.

Maugham instantly regretted his decision. Syrie was ill-read, ill-bred, and a spendthrift. Syrie felt neglected both in and out of the bedroom. By 1929 they were divorced, with Maugham forced to pay Syrie £2,400 a year until she remarried.

She never did, so Maugham kept paying for his lapse until her death in 1955. His verdict on the marriage was succinct: "She had me every which way from the beginning and never ceased to give me hell."

---

Maugham's venom against Syrie exploded late in his life when he published "Looking Back," a series of articles attacking her and claiming that their daughter was not his. Friends of Syrie lashed back. One wrote that Syrie had loved Maugham for himself "with his stumpy little body, his trembling lips, and his shimmering contorted brain."

---

# Hemingway's Honeymoon (1921)

He was twenty-one and her "Hasovitch"; she was twenty-nine and his "Nesto." During their nine-month courtship, they exchanged hundreds of letters but saw each other only seven times, so it must have been a shock for newlywed Hadley Hemingway to glimpse the true nature of her newly minted husband, Ernest.

They were married at Horton Bay in northern Michigan and, after the ceremony, were dropped off at Lake Walloon, near the island where the Hemingway family had their summer home.

The honeymoon got off to a rocky start when the couple fell ill and the weather turned cold. When Ernest wasn't working on his stories, they stayed indoors and nursed their fevers with mulled wine.

One morning, Ernest crossed the lake and hitchhiked into Horton Bay for supplies. He bought a four-pound steak, recovered from a friend his old army uniform, and got stinking drunk with a friendly bootlegger.

Staggering to the shore, he "borrowed" a friend's motorboat and sped off for the cabin. Hearing Ernest's shouts, Hadley walked down to the water's edge in time to see her drunken husband roaring by on the choppy waters. He tossed the steak at her, waved, and drove off up the coast.

Hadley walked through the woods until she could hear Ernest's voice. She found him wearing his uniform, still half-drunk and singing an Italian army song.

He also didn't endear himself to her by insisting on introducing her to his former girlfriends in nearby Petoskey. He explained he wanted to elevate him in her eyes, but she thought the exercise was a sop to his vanity and in bad taste.

The honeymoon, she admitted later, was "mostly a flop."

## Dashiell Hammett's Dirty Weekend (1931)

When it came to women, mystery writer and *Maltese Falcon* author Dashiell Hammett did what he wanted, no matter what anyone thought. Even when he was passionately in love with playwright Lillian Hellman, they fought regularly and were not wholly loyal to each other. Seven months into their relationship, Lillian had an affair with magazine editor Ralph Ingersoll and Dash fell in love with the humorist S. J. Perelman's wife, Laura.

Matters came to a head at a Fourth of July party he threw at his house in Bel Air. Among the guests were Sid and Laura, plus several Chinese prostitutes from Hammett's favorite whorehouse, Madame Lee Francis.

After the drinks were flowing, Hammett told one of the prostitutes to get undressed in the upstairs bathroom. He then sent Sid upstairs, and—after waiting to let nature take its course—suggested to Laura that she should see what Sid was up to. End of party.

Next, she agreed with Dash's suggestion that they spend the weekend in San Francisco. She had always been fond of him. But the weekend didn't turn out like they planned. Dash fell ill, and while he was fit enough for the bedroom, Laura realized that Dash wasn't going to leave Lillian for her.

Meanwhile, Lillian was beside herself with rage. Prostitutes were one thing, but running off with a friend was an insult to her. She raged at him when he returned, but his attitude with Lillian was like that with Laura: Hammett was going to do what he felt like doing. Like it or lump it.

Hammett and Hellman would remain partners for the rest of his life, but Lillian could neither forgive nor forget his betrayal. "I could kill him for that . . . even now," she said forty years after the party. "After all this time . . . I could still kill him. . . . I wish he were alive so I could kill him."

## Make Love the Samuel Beckett Way (1937)

For Peggy Guggenheim, it was love at first sight when she spotted Samuel Beckett at a dinner party in Paris. He was sitting beside James Joyce, already notorious for *Ulysses*, but Peggy had eyes only for the tall, lanky, bespectacled Irishman who, she thought, "always seemed to be far away solving some intellectual problem."

While he was unnerved by her stares, he surprised her by offering to walk her home, where they spent the night and most of the next day in bed. When they weren't making love, they drank and talked about art; his short-story collection *More Pricks Than Kicks*; and his unpublished novel *Murphy*. When Peggy mentioned that she loved champagne, he impulsively left her bed to buy several bottles.

He also surprised her again that evening. When she left him to keep a dinner engagement, he replied, "Thank you. It was nice while it was lasted."

So that was it, she thought, until they met on the street a few days later. They took to her bed again, this time for nearly two weeks.

The affair lasted thirteen months. She loved his unpredictability, never knowing when she would see him again, or how he would act toward her. He seemed to be either drunk, lost in his thoughts, or both.

But unpredictability had its limits. When Beckett slept with a friend of his visiting from Dublin, he explained to Peggy that he couldn't get rid of her any other way. Besides, he didn't love her, and "making love without being in love was like taking coffee without brandy." Peggy threw him out anyway.

> Beckett's attitude toward romance was demonstrated when he and Peggy stopped at a hotel for the night. He asked for a double room. Looking forward to a good time, Peggy jumped into bed naked, only to be told absolutely not.
>
> "Then why did you take the double room?" she demanded.
>
> Beckett shrugged. "It was cheaper."

# When Sylvia Bit Ted (1956)

To Ted Hughes, their meeting was as if "the solar system had married us." To Sylvia Plath, he was "as big as his poems." Their first meeting at a Cambridge University literary party was nothing short of mythic.

Plath was a Fulbright scholar studying at Cambridge and already a published writer, her poems and short stories appearing in magazines such as *Seventeen*, *Atlantic Monthly*, and *Mademoiselle*, where her experiences as a guest editor would resurface in her novel *The Bell Jar*.

# Altered States

Some writers had unconventional views about marriage:

- Wilkie Collins was a faithful if unorthodox husband. He took up with Mrs. Caroline Greaves in 1858, lived with her unmarried for nine years and adopted her daughter. When she left to marry another man, he turned to Martha Rudd, who bore him three children. But when Mrs. Greaves returned in 1870, he set her up in another household and she gave him another child. When he died in 1889, he recognized all four illegitimate children in his will.

- George Gissing didn't want a wife who was his social equal, so he turned to prostitutes. The first one he married in 1879 became bored with respectability and returned to the street. Gissing tried again in 1891 with a servant girl. He infected her with the syphilis he picked up from his first wife, and she was sent to an asylum.

- If anyone needed marrying, it was G. K. Chesterton, who needed a caretaker more than a wife. Fortunately, his wife, Frances, whom he married in 1901, willingly assumed the role of organizing his life. He would be so lost in thought that he'd forget his surroundings, even what he was supposed to do next. One time, during a lecture tour, he sent Frances a telegram: "Am in Birmingham. Where ought I be?"

- When Thomas Mann's daughter was ordered home to Nazi Germany in 1935, her life was at risk because of her father's anti-Nazi activities. So W. H. Auden agreed to marry her and make her a British subject. "After all," the homosexual Auden said, "what are buggers for?"

- When Dorothy Parker's husband, Alan Campbell, died in 1963, a friend asked what she could do for her. "Get me a new husband," she replied. "I think that is the most callous and disgusting remark I ever heard in my life," the friend said. Dottie sighed and said gently, "So sorry. Then run down to the corner and get me a ham and cheese on rye and tell them to hold the mayo."

At Cambridge, she discovered a new literary magazine co-founded by Hughes. Two years older, Hughes had graduated from Cambridge and was living in London, doing odd jobs and contemplating moving to Australia. He had not advanced nearly as far as Plath as a poet, but his poetry impressed her—particularly one about male competition that ended in a murder, with the killer "bursting into the police station / Crying . . . 'I did it, I.' "

So when the magazine held a party celebrating its first issue, Plath was there. When she spied the tall, handsome Hughes across the crowded, noisy room, she waved and cried out, "I did it, I!" "You like?" he called back. He took her to another room where, she wrote in her journal, he kissed her "bang smash on the mouth. I bit him long and hard on the cheek . . . blood was running down his face." After that breathless meeting, she reflected, "I can see how women lie down for artists."

Four months later, they were married.

# The Joy of Sex

Whether a woodland frolic or a back-
alley knee-trembler, writers get it
on for real.

## Boswell Goes Slumming (1763)

There was one thing that James Boswell loved more than sucking up to Samuel Johnson and taking notes of the Great Cham's bons mots, and that was sampling the delights of London—particularly its women.

On one particular night, to celebrate King George III's birthday, he dressed down in his "second-mourning suit, dirty buckskin breeches, black stockings, and a little round hat with tarnished silver lace belonging to a disbanded officer of the Royal Volunteers," and toddled off to his favorite hunting grounds, St. James Park.

Nowadays, St. James is a finely manicured lawn haunted by tourists and white pelicans that gather on the lake, but in his time, Boswell called it "a long dirty field, intersected by a wide dirty ditch." It was also incredibly fetid. If the smell of the rank grass and rotten lime trees didn't knock you out, the garbage dumped by the city's residents would.

But Boswell was made of sterner stuff, or of a weaker nose. In St. James, he wrote, he "picked up a low brimstone, agreed with her for sixpence, went to the bottom of the Park and dipped my machine in the Canal and performed most manfully."

Next, "roaring along" the street, he stopped at Ashley's Punch-house and got drunk. Then he walked to The Strand, where another negotiation turned unexpectedly risky.

> I picked up a little profligate and gave her 6 pence. She allowed me entrance. But the miscreant refused me performance. I was much stronger than her, and *volens nolens* [willy-nilly] pushed her up against the way. She however gave a sudden spring from me; and screaming out, a parcel of more whores and soldiers came to her relief.

Thinking quickly, Boswell called out, "Brother soldiers, should not a half-pay officer roger for sixpence? And here has she used me so and so." That won over the crowd, and he "abused her in blackguard style" and toddled off.

He returned home at two in the morning, intoxicated with his sport and gratified that "notwithstanding my dress, I was always taken for a gentleman in disguise."

Boswell cut a wide swath through the female half of London society. According to his diaries, by the time he was twenty-nine, he had tried to seduce a dozen highborn ladies, acquired a nearly equal number of mistresses, and had sex with over sixty prostitutes. He also contracted gonorrhea seventeen times.

## Dictionary Johnson and Mrs. Thrale's Flail (1765)

When they met at a dinner party in 1765, Samuel "Dictionary" Johnson was fifty-four and one of London's leading literary figures. Hester Thrale was a vivacious, twenty-four-year-old woman unhappily married to a cold, philandering brewer. For nineteen years, she and the wordsmith formed a unique bond, possibly in more ways than one.

Hester adored Johnson's wit, even if it meant enduring his scarred face, convulsive gestures, tremors, and frequent depressions. Johnson was equally besotted, and in a letter he begged her to "keep me in that form of slavery which you know so well how to make blissful."

"Of all the unhappy you were the happiest," she replied coyly, "in consequence of my Attention to your Complaint."

"Says Johnson," she remembered after his death, "a Woman has such power between the Ages of twenty five and forty five, that She may tye a Man to a post and whip him if She will." In a footnote, she added, "This he knew of him self was literally and strictly true."

Another time, she wrote that often the doctor not only kissed her hand "ay and my foot too upon his knees! Strange Connections there are in this odd World!"

So close was their relationship that, when her husband died, many expected them to marry. Instead, she chose Gabriel Mario Piozzi, an Italian musician who had taught her daughters, and planned to leave for Europe.

London society was scandalized that she would marry a foreigner. Johnson was enraged that she would leave him. He begged her to stay in England, but she left for Italy with her new husband.

After playing baby maker to her husband and disciplinarian to her friend, Hester thrived with her music teacher. But she never forgot Johnson, who died five months after she announced her marriage. Among her effects after her death was a memento, the meaning of which biographers still argue over: an item labeled "Johnson's padlock."

# A Cougar Traps Bernard Shaw (1885)

While George Bernard Shaw's marriage to Charlotte Payne-Townshend in 1898 was never consummated, that didn't make the playwright a forty-two-year-old virgin.

When he was a poor twenty-eight-year-old failed novelist and budding socialist, he met Mrs. Jenny Patterson. The tall, red-bearded Irishman found himself drawn to the forty-four-year-old widow with the fiery temper and "remarkable bust."

For months, Shaw would call on Mrs. Patterson in the evening for what he called "supper, music and curious conversation." He desired her, but he was too fastidious when it came to sex. Just examining a packet of condoms he bought, he wrote in his diary, "extraordinarily revolted me." Nevertheless, he marked his twenty-ninth birthday with "a new experience" when Jenny took him to her bed.

But it was not a happy relationship. Lonely and sex-starved, Shaw couldn't resist her seductions. Away from her, he'd feel guilty and mortified over his lack of control. "I wanted to love," he wrote, "but not to be appropriated." For several years, he tried to end their relationship, but their attempts to be just friends reverted too often to being friends with benefits.

Then in 1893, Shaw, now a rising playwright, began spending time with actress Florence Farr. A jealous Jenny began creating scenes. The arguments grew more frequent, and she'd sneak into his rooms and steal his letters to Florence.

One evening, while Shaw was with his new friend, Jenny burst in on them. The arguing and recriminations grew so violent that Shaw sent Florence away for her protection. He stayed behind, walked Jenny home, and calmed her with his talk. He didn't get home until 4 a.m.

Jenny apologized, but this time the break was permanent. By the time he got married, Shaw fervently believed that sex was something that should only happen to other people.

## Wilde Dines Out (1897)

After his release from jail, Oscar Wilde went into exile in France, where he was tempted into visiting a brothel in Dieppe with unhappy results.

According to William Butler Yeats, a friend had impressed on Wilde "the necessity of acquiring 'a more wholesome taste.'" At a café, while they pooled their money, word spread that Wilde was in town, so by the time they stepped out to visit a brothel, they were followed by a cheerful crowd.

At their destination, Wilde went inside, and everyone awaited his return. When he appeared, he said quietly to his friend, "The first in ten years, and it will be the last. It was like cold mutton." Then aloud, so that the crowd might hear him, "But tell it in England, for it will entirely restore my character."

## Kafka's Kurious Kollection (1900s)

The literary world was rocked in 2008 by news that the author of *The Metamorphosis* had a taste for the stuff for which the Internet was created—porn.

Not that it was a big surprise to the Kafka scholars. They had known for decades that he kept obscene materials in a locked cabinet in the home he shared with his parents. It was just considered bad form to talk about it, much less link it with his writings.

In fact, unlike his image as a secular saint, Kafka was a rake. His diaries contain frequent mentions of his adventures with ladies of negotiable virtue, visits which he usually shared with his good friend Max Brod. In one letter he proposed to Max an evening out, ending with hitting the cafés after 5 a.m. and having their girls "as an early breakfast."

A prurient interest in sex also links Kafka to Franz Blei, the Fontane Prize judge who pulled strings to give Kafka a boost early in his career (see "Kafka Gets a Little Help from His Friends," on page 31). Kafka subscribed to Blei's limited-edition "journal," which was the *Penthouse* of its day, if *Penthouse* printed deeply weird artwork, such as a hairy frog-like creature performing fellatio on phallic-looking mushrooms. Kafka was an eager reader; when one issue was late, he moaned to Blei: "Why is God punishing Blei, Germany, and us? And especially me?"

Kafka's interest in erotica was not limited to his friend's output. He also bought Octave Mirbeau's *Sin and Other Stories* and *Revelations of a Chambermaid* and had read Leopold von Sacher-Masoch's *Venus in Furs*. The prize of the collection was probably Blei's edition of Lucian's *Conversations of the Courtesans*, with its fifteen pictures of what would be called today "hot girl-on-girl" action by Gustav Klimt. A copy of that edition would set you back several thousand dollars today.

---

Kafka even inserted an in-joke in *The Castle* to amuse his friends. Pepi, the barmaid who offers herself to Josef K., shares her name with the serving-girl heroine in a soft-porn romance written by Brod and published by Blei.

# H. G. Wells's Threesome (1910)

One of literature's great horn dogs, H. G. Wells managed to combine a Clintonian nose for women, a compliant wife, and an ability to avoid scandal (with one exception; see "Wells and the Angry Hedwig," on page 197).

One of his affairs was with Elizabeth von Arnim, the cousin of Katherine Mansfield and the bestselling author of *Elizabeth and Her German Garden*, her charming memoir about life on a country estate. After her divorce and move to Switzerland, she welcomed frequent visits from Wells to her chalet. They would spend their mornings writing, and their afternoons walking through the fields and woods. At night, Wells could open the secret door between their rooms for some nocturnal nookie.

One day, while on a picnic, they read in the *London Times* a letter from the elderly novelist Mrs. Humphry Ward attacking the moral code of the younger generation of writers, in particular Rebecca West, a journalist who, too, would become a Wells paramour.

Wells and von Arnim responded to her letter by spreading out the *Times*, getting naked and, as Wells wrote, making love "all over Mrs. Humphry Ward." Then they burned the newspaper.

# Hemingway After Dark (1920s)

Ernest Hemingway's writing may have exemplified modernism, but his attitude toward sex was firmly rooted in the age of Victoria. He believed that a man had a limited number of orgasms that should be rationed throughout his life. He also believed in marriage, going to the altar four times and always having the next wife in line while he was divorcing the previous one.

William Faulkner, who kept the same wife but carried on numerous affairs, summed up Papa's philosophy best: "Hemingway's mistake was that he thought he had to marry all of them."

But while Hemingway was all man when it came to hunting, fishing, boxing, and bullfighting, it appears he came up short in the sack. Part of his problem stemmed from his drinking, which caused impotence that grew worse over the years. But his first wife, Hadley, thought that Ernest was simply too distracted to be a good lover. In the middle of making love, she said, he would grab a book from the bedside table and read it over her shoulder. That's enough to throw any woman off her stride.

## Mary McCarthy's First Time (1926)

After her parents died in the 1918 flu epidemic, Mary McCarthy was sent to live with her grandparents in Seattle. For years, their control over her life was absolute, especially where boys were concerned. She'd sneak out of the house and lie to them while she looked for opportunities to break free.

So when twenty-seven-year-old college graduate Forrest Crosby, with his close-cut curly hair, navy blue jacket, and pipe, wanted to make love to her, she was willing. She was also fourteen.

First, they tried on the sofa in her grandparents' living room, but Forrest fled when someone came to the door. Then Mary was sent to a seminary, so their next opportunity came a few months later when she came home over Thanksgiving.

Decades later, McCarthy could still recall the scene. She met Forrest one chilly night in the front seat of his Marmon roadster that was parked on an isolated street. Forrest began his seduction by talking about a girl from the seminary who was seduced by one of his friends. Then he unbuttoned himself to show her what an erect penis looked like—"quite repellent, all flushed and purplish," she remembered—and pulled out a condom and rolled it on while lecturing about its purpose.

She remembered little of the intercourse except for "a slight sense of being stuffed." Afterward, there was "a single dreadful, dazed moment" when Crosby held the condom up to the streetlight so she could see the ejaculate.

Whether because of desperation or optimism, Mary agreed to meet Crosby again. She showed up, but he didn't. She returned the next night with the same result. They exchanged brief notes before he dumped her with an unsigned note.

What a lover.

> **McCarthy was fascinated with men throughout her life. When she was between husbands in the 1930s, she entertained a succession of men in her one-room apartment. When she realized one day that she had slept with three men in twenty-four hours, she admitted in her memoirs being "slightly scared," but that she "did not feel promiscuous."**

## Anaïs and Henry and Hugo (1932)

While Anaïs Nin enjoyed her affair with Henry Miller, she felt guilty about betraying her husband Hugo. So she did what any wife would do to make it up to her husband: She took him to a brothel.

So on Saturday night, Anaïs and Hugo stepped out for dinner and an unusual floor show at a high-quality house Henry recommended that specialized in voyeurs. After learning the house did not offer a man and a woman, Anaïs chose two women—one heavy and

Spanish-looking and the other small and timid—and they sat at a table and made small talk over drinks. The ladies, naked except for their shawls, discussed each other's nails and praised Anaïs's choice of "nacreous" polish.

Then they went upstairs. The girls performed a variety of poses using dildoes, then Anaïs asked them to show some "lesbian poses." When the larger woman brought the smaller one to orgasm, Anaïs discovered what a clitoris was for. She encouraged Hugo to join them, but he declined.

The couple went home and made violent love, and while Anaïs thought the evening went well, Hugo suffered a stress-related illness. When it came to sex in their marriage, Anaïs learned she was the pioneer. Her husband preferred to stay home.

## Dylan Thomas Chases Shirley Jackson (1950)

During his poetry tour of America, Dylan Thomas preferred a direct approach to seduction, asking the college girls that flocked about him, "Can I jump you?"

Most of the time, it worked. One time it didn't was during a visit to the Connecticut home of writer Shirley Jackson and her husband, Stanley.

By this time of his life, Thomas was tubby with thinning hair and reeked of alcohol and cigarettes, both of which he consumed in great quantities; a shade of the Welsh romantic who had set hearts fluttering. Jackson was hardly the seducible type, either, being overweight and also a heavy drinker.

After the threesome spent the evening discussing literature over several bottles, Stanley excused himself to catch a night baseball game on the TV. Sitting on the couch next to her, Dylan popped the question. We don't know what Shirley said, but he seemed to take it as a yes. We don't know what Dylan did, but Shirley fled the room with him close on her heels.

Shirley ran up the stairs, down the hall, down the back stairs, and through the room between her husband and the national pastime. Fueled by the alcohol, Dylan kept pace, so they ran the circuit again. And again. Stanley finally put a stop to the Tour de Jackson when he grabbed Dylan by his belt. The poet hit the floor, and Shirley escaped.

## Erica Jong's Bargain (1973)

There are many negotiating tactics in the book business, but Erica Jong discovered one presumably rarely used between writers and publishers.

Before her debut novel *Fear of Flying* introduced "zipless fuck" into the lexicon, Jong was invited to lunch by an elderly publisher. As they ate at the Algonquin, he ran his fingers up her thigh, praised her poetry, and asked how much she wanted for her novel. She impulsively said a half million. He accepted.

After lunch, he took her to his office to show her his book collection. She swooned at the sight of first editions of John Keats's *Endymion* and Walt Whitman's *Leaves of Grass*. As she did, he embraced her from behind then turned her around for a kiss. All too quickly, she found herself on her knees, and in return for delivering his happy ending, hoped for one of his first editions.

But it was all for naught. Not only did the publisher pass on the novel, but he sent her a copy of *Leaves of Grass* that was a facsimile first edition. Jong felt betrayed—"I didn't give him a facsimile blow job!"—but she did gain a measure of revenge

# Writers on Sex

- Honoré de Balzac believed that his creativity required that he keep his semen to himself. When one seduction led to its natural conclusion, he cried to his friends in 1831, "I lost a book this morning!" He told Alexandre Dumas *fils* that no woman was worth two volumes a year.
- Victor Hugo believed the sex and genius were linked, and both needed to be exercised as often as possible. In 1847, when his son asked him to intercede with his unfaithful lover, Alice Ozy, Hugo solved his son's problem by seducing her.
- Alexandre Dumas *pere*, like Hugo, had no truck with Balzac's nonsense. "If you locked me in my bedroom with five women, pens, paper, ink and a play to be written," he boasted in 1861, "by the end of an hour I'd have written the play and had the five women."
- Like any well-brought-up lady of her time, Edith Wharton was ignorant of bedroom activities. Before her wedding in 1885, when she delicately asked her mother "what being married was like," she was told, "I never heard such a ridiculous question."
- Leo Tolstoy found no relief in sex, and throughout his life tortured himself between his desire and his self-loathing. His wife suffered as well, giving birth to their last child—their thirteenth—when she was forty-four and he was sixty. "Marriage cannot cause happiness," he fulminated in 1899. "It is always torture, which man has to pay for satisfying his sex urge."

by describing in her memoir *Seducing the Demon* his, ahem, shortcomings.

> When Erica Jong shocked America by writing about the zipless fuck in *Fear of Flying*, she was presented with a curious problem. She asked her friend, confessional poet Anne Sexton, for advice about what to do if a man asked her for one. "Thank them," Sexton said, "and say, 'Zip up your fuck until I ask for it.'"

·17·

# The End of the Affair

*It's the same old story: She done him
wrong, because he had it coming.*

## The Lamb Became a Tiger (1812)

When Lady Caroline Lamb met Lord Byron, she predicted that his "beautiful pale face is my fate." She didn't want to just love Byron; she wanted to become him. She dressed like a page boy to amuse him and published poetry that mimicked his style. She forged his handwriting so well that it fooled his publisher, John Murray, into sending her a miniature of the poet intended for a rival lover.

She had an equal effect on Byron, who described her as "a little volcano . . . the cleverest most agreeable, absurd, amiable, perplexing, dangerous, fascinating little being that lives." He was, in her famous words, "mad, bad and dangerous to know," but it applied to her as well, especially after he dumped her.

She tried to lure him back, and was rejected by him and mocked by society, so she avenged herself by writing *Glenarvon*, a Gothic romance in which Byron is thinly disguised as the satanic villain. The roman à clef was a bestseller, but it ostracized her from high society and strained relations with her husband, who was not amused at his portrayal as a cuckold.

As for Byron, he drily commented: "If the authoress had written the truth . . . the romance would not only have been more romantic, but more entertaining. As for the likeness, the picture can't be good—I did not sit long enough." But she had left her mark on him. When a lady had the temerity to dump him, he complained that it left him feeling "Carolinish."

Of his many affairs with both sexes, and even with his half sister, Augusta, Byron by far preferred teenage boys. But he had to be careful expressing his desire. Before publishing his love poems, he carefully changed the pronouns from masculine to feminine.

## George Sand's One-Night Stand (1833)

The brief affair between the novelist George Sand and Prosper Mérimée was probably the most disastrous one-night stand in literature, and it played out before all of Paris.

Although twenty-nine years old and living on her own as a successful writer, Sand was no Carrie Bradshaw. She was estranged from her husband and, with her son in boarding school, was notorious for her affairs. The gossipers on the Left Bank were shocked and amused at her habit of wearing men's clothes and smoking cigs she rolled herself. She was also a detached lover. The gossipy Goncourt brothers noted in their diary that she possessed "a basic coldness which allowed her to write about her lovers when practically in bed with them."

Then Marie Dorval upset her ordered world. Sand fell hard for the beautiful actress and didn't care that she was a lesbian (although she didn't consider herself one). When she wasn't spending her evenings with Dorval, she threw her energies and frustrations into her third novel, *Lélia*, which, not coincidentally, was about a woman's struggles to find satisfaction in her relationships.

When her friends read her work in progress, they concluded that Sand needed a man to get her groove back. Mérimée, an archaeologist, epicurean, and writer whose *Carmen* would become an opera, was thought the ideal candidate. Sand, at first, agreed. She thought he was a strong man "who laughed at my sorrows [and] knew the secret of happiness." Soon they were seen in public. The sight of them leaving the theater, with her son asleep on Prosper's shoulder, amused the boulevardiers, who wondered if he was becoming domesticated.

By the end of one week, however, George and Prosper were getting along like oil and water. She treated sex with the passion of a tax audit, and in their one attempt at bed play, he wilted under her cool stare and indifference. When she suggested another meeting, he rejected her in a curt note: "You have the tone of a young girl without her advantages, and the pride of a marquise with none of her graces."

"Mérimée and I shouted and cursed each other as the wives of fishmongers would if they possessed larger, more imaginative vocabularies," she wrote to Gustave Flaubert. "We devoted ourselves exclusively to insults and hurtful remarks, and not once in the entire week did either of us address a civil comment to the other."

Meanwhile, literary Paris dissected the rumors, including that Mérimée insulted Sand by leaving a 5-franc piece on her dresser. Alexandre Dumas decided that Mérimée was upset because he wasn't up to the task of loving Sand. "What do you expect?" he crowed. "Mérimée is five feet, five inches tall."

Sand was devastated. While she never said, "I had Mérimée last night, it was nothing out of the ordinary"—she blamed Dumas for coining that phrase—she did write that "I cried with pain, disgust and despair. Instead of finding a friendship that would allow me to unburden my feelings of resentment and discouragement, I found only bitter and frivolous mockery."

> Sand was admired not only for her novels but also for something more, well, fundamental. "Madame Sand," the critic Sainte-Beuve said, "has a great soul and a perfectly enormous bottom." But this admiration had a down side. Arguing with her sculptor son-in-law, she screamed, "I'll publish an account of your behavior." He shot back: "Then I'll do a carving of your backside, and everybody'll recognize it!"

## Rimbaud: "You Really Look Like a Dick!" (1873)

Arthur Rimbaud was young and beautiful, with "the perfectly oval face of an angel in exile." Paul Verlaine was an older, bourgeoisie, married man who looked like "an orangutan escaped from the zoo." When Verlaine took the promising young poet from the provinces under his wing, it couldn't have been a match made in heaven because they raised too much hell.

Both poets were nasty pieces of work. Rimbaud had a genius for abusing hospitality: sunbathing in the nude, spreading his body lice, destroying his host's prized possessions, and leaving behind squalor. Verlaine, behind his facade of bourgeoisie respectability, was a brutal husband, frequently drunk, and abusive to his wife and child.

Together, they scandalized Paris with their drinking and drug taking, while writing the poetry that would make them famous. When the city got too hot for them, Verlaine abandoned his relieved if newly impoverished family, and fled town with Rimbaud to London, where the combustible couple would break up over a bizarre incident.

They were living in poverty in the Camden area, and Verlaine had gone shopping for lunch. From his window at the top of the house, Rimbaud saw his lover returning with two kippers, holding them before him at arm's length. Bursting into a laugh, Rimbaud shouted, *"Ce que tu as l'air con!"* (You really look like a dick!)

Without a word, Verlaine walked upstairs, packed, and left. The fate of the kippers is unknown.

They reunited in Brussels a week later, but it was all squabbling and drinking, and it ended badly when Verlaine shot Rimbaud in the wrist, for which he was given two years at hard labor. After he got out, he tracked down his lover—Dorothy Parker cracked that "he was always chasing Rimbauds"—but the magic was gone. After more fighting, Verlaine left Rimbaud forever. Soon, Rimbaud would leave poetry and pursue making money (see "Rimbaud the Gun Runner," on page 72).

## Edith Wharton Unleashed (1907)

For Edith Wharton, 1907 marked a year of liberation for her, both in her art and in her life.

At the start of the year, she felt trapped in her failing, loveless marriage to Teddy Wharton and there seemed little chance of that changing. Then they moved to Paris, a city she loved, and while Teddy traveled on business, she sought out friends with the "ineradicable passion for good talk."

One of them was Morton Fullerton, the expatriate American and correspondent for the *London Times* who became her closest friend. He was charming and knowledgeable about French politics, culture, and people. He was also very attractive with a flamboyant moustache and intense blue eyes.

Teddy's frequent trips away threw Edith and Morton together. They explored the neighborhoods of Paris and toured the medieval villages in the countryside. They made love in the inns. For a woman who wrote that sex with her husband of twelve years was "agonized," Morton's touch was ecstasy.

At age thirty-five, she wrote, "I have drunk of the wine of life at last." She added, "I have known the thing best worth knowing."

But Morton was feckless. Edith learned that he had had affairs with both men and women, and had been on intimate terms with Oscar Wilde. Not only had he been married but he was even engaged to his cousin, who had grown up believing they were brother and sister. As she grew closer to him, he pulled away, leaving her notes unanswered. Edith began suspecting that to him, she was "a 'course' served and cleared away!"

She went out of her way to help him. When he complained of feeling trapped in journalism, she promoted his work to publishers and suggested that he write a book about Paris. When his mistress blackmailed him, Edith and Henry James convinced a publisher to give Morton a book advance to pay her off that was really drawn from Edith's royalty account.

After three years of tearful separations and tender reconciliations, Wharton admitted defeat. She and Morton would remain friends, but the relationship was over. While she still loved him, she understood that the man's greatest accomplishment was "that exquisite art in him of not bringing it off."

## Upton Sinclair's "Great Tragedy" (1911)

As a socialist and muckraker, Upton Sinclair understood political systems. Human feelings, however, flummoxed him, especially the behavior of women, whom he saw as either goddesses or demons.

This especially applied to Meta, his wife. Although they had known each other since childhood, they never understood that they were incompatible as a couple until they were married. She was passionate; he was prim, even humorless. She was emotional where he was intellectual.

Their marriage had been faltering by the time they had moved to Arden, a village near Wilmington, Delaware, so Sinclair welcomed a distraction in the form of a visit from Harry Kemp. The tramp poet had presented himself as Sinclair's most ardent fan, calling their friendship "almost like the love of God." Sinclair saw Kemp as devoted solely to poetry and a man who didn't drink, smoke, and chase women. It turns out he was right about two of those things.

Sinclair and Kemp bonded during their long walks in the woods around Arden, where they talked about their work, their lives, and women. Sinclair favored affairs outside marriage and advised Kemp to avoid delicate women who needed men too much. He confessed that his marriage to Meta was breaking up.

Then, Sinclair and ten others were arrested for playing baseball on a Sunday. While he served an eighteen-hour sentence in the workhouse, Kemp took Meta for a long walk in the woods. That must have been a bracing walk: a few days later, Sinclair looked through the window of a neighboring cabin and saw Kemp and Meta making love.

The news that *The Jungle*'s author was filing for divorce caused headlines nationwide. Sinclair was called a hypocrite for advocating affairs and then kicking his wife out for practicing what he preached.

Meta told the reporters that she was a "varietist" and that she didn't "give a damn about marriage, divorce" or anything else except Harry. Sinclair used his notoriety to advocate welfare for mothers, but privately, he felt like he was being flayed alive.

To cap Sinclair's humiliation, the New York Supreme Court refused to grant a divorce on the grounds that he encouraged the adultery. He had to go to Holland to get one, ending—no doubt with some relief—what he called "the great tragedy of my life."

## Harold and Vita and Violet and Denys (1920)

Vita Sackville-West and Violet Keppel were in love, but what started with passion in England turned into a farce in France.

They had played together as children, and grew closer as they grew up. They were so close that after Vita married Harold Nicholson and Violet married Denys Trefusis, they promised that they wouldn't go to bed with their husbands. While Denys reluctantly agreed to this, Harold was content, so long as Vita left him to his affairs with men.

But Violet wanted more from Vita; she wanted to elope and live with her lover. Vita loved her life with Harold, but she loved Violet's "quivering flesh, the kisses of your mouth, and the caresses of your fingers." Her feelings in turmoil, she agreed to leave her husband, and together they plotted their journey to France.

At Dover, while Violet crossed the English Channel, Vita stayed behind a day, only to encounter a pursuing Denys. His misery softened Vita's heart so much that she agreed to help him get Violet back.

They found Violet in Amiens, where she again rejected Denys. In despair, he agreed to a separation and left for London. But before they could head on to Paris, Violet's father caught up with them and refused to let them go until Denys came back. For two days, he stayed at the hotel while Vita and Violet played tourist.

Meanwhile, in London, Denys met Harold and told him what his wife was up to. This roused the normally complacent man; having affairs were one thing, but running off to France crossed the line. They hired a two-seater airplane, and Denys flew them back to Amiens.

At the hotel, the men ordered their wives to pack and come home with them. The wives refused, and as they all argued, Harold dropped his bombshell: Violet had gone to bed with Denys.

Stunned, Vita asked Denys, then Violet, if it was true. Gentleman to the core, Denys refused to answer, and Violet didn't deny it. Feeling the world shift beneath her, Vita capitulated and went back to Harold.

---

Another of Vita's great loves was with novelist Virginia Woolf, who would immortalize her in her novel, *Orlando*. When Virginia visited Vita for three days, Leonard Woolf sent a note asking Vita to make sure his wife goes to bed "not 1 minute later than 11 p.m. and that she doesn't talk too long at a time."

---

# Wells and the Angry Hedwig (1923)

H. G. Wells's life was notable not only for his range of works—*The War of the Worlds*, *The Invisible Man*, *The Time Machine*, and *The Outline of History*—but for his range of women. The self-styled "Don Juan among the intelligentsia" not only supported a wife and family but sired children by at least two mistresses and bedded many more, including novelist Elizabeth von Arnim (see "H. G. Wells's Threesome," on page 182).

The most committed of Wells's relationships was with Rebecca West. The journalist had panned one of his novels, calling him "an old maid among novelists." He responded by inviting her to tea and a seduction. The affair would eventually result in a son, Anthony West.

However, two women were not enough. In 1923, Wells began seeing Hedwig Verena Gatternigg, a fan and his Austrian translator. But when she became too serious about their affair, Wells ended it.

A distraught Hedwig visited Rebecca to complain. When she understandably refused to help, Hedwig invaded Wells's London apartment, nearly naked under her raincoat, and threatened to kill herself. While Wells fled to fetch help, she slashed her wrists and armpits, leaving a bloody mess on the floor and Wells's shirtfront.

She survived, and the newspapers had a field day with the story, although Wells was able, through his connections with the newspaper barons, to suppress his connection with Gatternigg. Repairing relations with West wasn't as successful. He tried to pass Hedwig off as "a gnawing, incessant little rat, threatening all my peace with you," but the damage was done. Wells, she concluded, "treated me with the sharpest cruelty imaginable for those horrible years," and her son would grow up to resent his mother and idolize his absent father.

As for Wells, it rankled him more that West still didn't like his novels. Instead, he harrumphed, she exalted "James Joyce and D. H. Lawrence, as if in defiance of me."


# The Mystery of the Disappearing Writer (1926)

On the surface, Agatha Christie lived the dream life of a bestselling author, with a loving husband, a daughter, and a home in the country. But underneath, the creator of Inspector Hercule Poirot would soon create a mystery that still haunts her fans.

At thirty-six, Christie was feeling as if her life was coming apart at the seams. Her mother had died, and in addition to running her household, writing stories, and raising her daughter, she had to settle her mother's estate and empty the family home. Furthermore, her self-centered husband, Archie, was emotionally distant and couldn't bear to be around his wife when she was stressed.

Then, Archie dropped a bombshell: he was in love with another woman and wanted a divorce. Agatha refused. The publicity would be humiliating, an admission that she had failed. Archie insisted. She ate badly and slept poorly. She seemed to lose her grip on reality. Once, she caught herself signing a check with a fictional character's name.

Then one afternoon, Archie and Agatha had a terrible argument, and he stalked off to spend the weekend with his mistress. That night, Agatha packed a bag and fled, leaving her daughter in the maid's care.

Police found her abandoned car the next day. The tabloids went wild, reporting every possible sighting and engaging in endless speculation. A nearby pond was dragged, and Archie found himself under suspicion, the target of rumors and innuendoes.

Eleven days later, Agatha surfaced at a hotel two hundred miles away in North Yorkshire, where she had been staying under the name of her husband's mistress. She claimed she had amnesia, which nobody believed. Two years later, she and Archie were divorced.

Publicity stunt? Nervous breakdown? Revenge? Biographers still argue over Agatha's motivations, but it seems Archie got off lucky. It's risky to cross a mystery writer known for her cunning plots and knowledge of poisons.

## The Frog That Ate the Crocodile (1963)

Their affair played out like a highbrow version of *The Odd Couple*. She was the Paris intellectual who advocated existentialism and feminism; he was the roughneck Chicago novelist comfortable behind a bottle or a poker hand.

Simone de Beauvoir was visiting Chicago when she called Nelson Algren and asked him to show her the city. Algren opened her eyes to the seamy side of American life, showing her the city's working-class bars, jazz clubs, burlesque shows, the prison's electric chair, and eventually, his bed.

Sex with Algren was electrifying and eye-opening. For the first time, she experienced an orgasm. She fell passionately in love with him. For two years, they exchanged letters and books. He gave her a ring and called her his "frog wife." She wore it and called him her "crocodile." They traveled down the Mississippi by riverboat to New Orleans. Crossing to Central America by ship, they swam in a lake formed by a volcano and, in their hotel room, sat naked by the fire, drinking whisky and telling stories.

He wanted to marry her, but she had bound herself to Jean-Paul Sartre, who needed her to edit his work and find him his mistresses. While Algren hated the arrangement, it suited Sartre well. When he didn't need de Beauvoir, he let her visit Nelson and called her back when he needed her again.

Eventually, after many fights, and with another lover on her string, Simone dropped Algren. But she wasn't through with him. She recast her romance with him in a novel, and in 1963, the third volume of her autobiography described her affair with Algren as something less than passionate and quoted from his letters.

A humiliated Algren fought back. "She's fantasizing a relationship in the manner of a middle-aged spinster," he told an interviewer.

"It was mostly a friendship. . . . It was casual." He never forgave her. She never forgot him. When she died, she was buried wearing his ring.

---

# When Love Turns Gray

- Breaking up is not always hard to do. When author and feminist Charlotte Perkins Gilman left painter Charles Walter Stetson in 1888, she wrote to tell him that, despite being "the greatest man" she ever knew, "I haven't felt unhappy once since I left. The fogs and mists are rolling away; I begin to feel alive and self-respecting. Oh the difference!"
- When Dada artist Baroness Elsa von Freytag-Loringhoven punched poet William Carlos Williams in 1921 for rejecting her advances—she had hidden in the backseat of his car and ambushed him, moaning, "Villiam Carlos Villiams, I vant you!"—he prepared for a rematch by training on a punching bag. When she attacked him again on Park Avenue, he said that he "flattened her with a stiff punch to the mouth" and had her arrested.
- At the Yaddo artists' colony in 1941, Carson McCullers was so powerfully drawn to Katherine Anne Porter that she spent hours outside her door, begging to be let in. At dinnertime, Porter opened the door, saw the prostrate McCullers on her threshold, and stepped over her without a word.
- When Kingsley Amis told his wife in 1963 of his plan to take his lover to Spain for the summer, she did not take it well. As he slept on the beach one afternoon, she used her lipstick to write "I fuck anything" on his bare back while their friends took photos. They were divorced two years later.

# 18

# Alcohol and Drugs

For inspiration or intoxication, they
risked a high price for getting high.

## Writer's Blockage (1804)

Samuel Taylor Coleridge's lifelong addiction to opium took a hor-
rific toll on his health. Not only did it cause insomnia, nightmares,
and frightening visions, but it caused colon paralysis leading to con-
stipation that was treated with enemas.

Normally, Coleridge enjoyed a good enema. But during a voyage
from England to Malta, complications set in that caused a "day of
Horror."

As Coleridge would recount, he began with a milder treatment
in which he sat over a bowl of hot water: "After two long frightful,
fruitless struggles, the face convulsed, & sweat streaming from me
like Rain, the Captn. Proposed to send for the Commadore's Surgeon. . . . The Surgeon instantly came, went back for Pipe & Syringe &
returned & with extreme difficulty & the exertion of his utmost
strength injected the latter."

But instead of the enema causing the blockage to soften,
"Good God! What a sensation when the obstruction suddenly *shot*

up!—I remained still three-quarters of an hour with hot water in a bottle to my belly . . . with pain & Sore uneasiness, & indescribable desires."

But there was worse to come as Coleridge "*picked out* the hardened matter & after *awhile* was completely relieved. The poor mate who stood by me all this while had the tears running down his face."

---

Coleridge's addiction to opium took the form of laudanum, a liquid tincture popularly sold as a nostrum for many illnesses. While it might have inspired many of his great early works such as "The Rime of the Ancient Mariner" and "Kubla Khan," repeated abuse killed his talent and left him near the end of his life a frail skeleton.

---

# O'Neill Meets the Green Fairy (1907)

Eugene O'Neill spent only one year at Princeton University, but he left an indelible impression.

At eighteen, he presented a startling sight: thin to the point of tubercular, broad-shouldered and wearing the traditional freshman's black beanie. He kept to himself, ignored his studies, and spent his time reading deeply into Shakespeare, Bernard Shaw, Lord Byron, Kipling, and the romantic poets.

He had also seen more of the world than most freshmen. He drank hard liquor, shocking the students used to beer and light wine. He proclaimed that he didn't believe in God and that women were whores, saying, "There is not such a thing as a virgin after the age of fourteen." He bragged about accompanying his brother to the bordellos in New York's Tenderloin district and proved it by taking classmates on a tour of his favorite spots.

But he went too far at the end of his first year. Curious about absinthe, he convinced a Greenwich Village friend, Louis Holladay, to bring a quart on his next visit. What he didn't know was that the liquor, nicknamed the "green fairy," had been banned in the United States because the wormwood used in its distillation caused hallucinations.

So absinthe did not make O'Neill's heart grow fonder, it drove him berserk. As Holladay watched in horror, O'Neill smashed a chair against a window frame, then wrenched off a chair leg and destroyed his washbowl and pitcher. He yanked out the drawers in his bureau and scattered their contents. While Holladay tried to calm him, O'Neill pawed through his belongings, found a revolver and aimed it at his friend. Fortunately for the future of American theater, it was unloaded.

Holladay fled, found O'Neill's friends, and brought them back to the rooms. It took three of them to hold him down and put him to bed, where he collapsed into a stupor.

The incident was hushed up, but when another incident led to a three-week suspension, O'Neill decided to part ways with Princeton.


## Katherine Anne Porter Tries to Fly (1921)

While living in Mexico, gathering material that would form her first collection of short stories, Katherine Anne Porter went on a memorable trip that was nearly fatal.

Sent from New York to write magazine articles, Porter was determined to absorb as much of Mexico as she could. She met a wide variety of people: expatriates like herself, Communists, European aristocrats with titles, artists, and Mexicans who were involved in various rebellions against the central government.

One night, she attended a party at an old colonial house that overlooked a ravine whose precipitous drop made her dizzy. There, she decided to try a local product called *la yerba encantadora*, known to us gringos as "marijuana."

It could have been her last trip. Either the marijuana was cut with hallucinogens or it reacted badly with Porter, because she felt herself coming unmoored from reality. As she moved through the crowd, their speech slowed as if she could hear the gaps between syllables. A man's skull changed into a crystalline dome, revealing gears and mechanisms pumping, turning, and whirling. With growing concern, she saw his lips still move, but the cogwheels stop.

As more domes began to appear on the guests, she walked nervously out onto the terrace. She saw shimmering stars caught in the branches of a dead jacaranda tree and felt serenity stealing over her. Gravity seemed optional. The night sky opened and looked so inviting that she climbed onto the balcony wall. If the guests hadn't held her back, she would have stepped off and fallen a hundred feet to the rocks below.

The next day, once the hangover passed, Porter found she had not only a memorable experience but the climax to "Flowering Judas," the short story that established her reputation.

## The DTs Dive-Bomb Faulkner (1936)

William Faulkner loved to talk about his combat experiences in Europe with the Canadian Flying Corps. He would tell how he got drunk and landed his plane upside down on top of the hangar, causing considerable damage to both plane and pilot. The accident, he would tell his listeners, left him in near-constant pain and walking with a limp. This is why he drank so much. His friends would come away amazed, not only by the story, but in Faulkner's amazing capacity to imbibe a lot of liquor without appearing drunk.

Truth be told, Faulkner was lying. He never got beyond ground school; he didn't even get to Europe before the war ended. The crash was just one of many tall tales he told, alongside the one about the two children he fathered in New Orleans and that he drank whisky made by the servants on his father's plantation.

To Faulkner, lying was as natural as breathing: "Any writer is a congenital liar to begin with or he wouldn't take up writing."

But as he neared forty, the effects of alcohol caught up with him. A steady drinker since he was fifteen, Faulkner had reached the point where he needed to drink around the clock. In the morning, he had to steady his hand against the wall to pour straight.

And when he had to go on the wagon to keep his job as a screenwriter at Twentieth Century-Fox, he began suffering from vivid hallucinations called delirium tremens, or DTs.

One morning, his lover, Meta Carpenter, awoke to find Faulkner crouching on their bed and screaming, "They're diving down at me. Swooping. Oh, Lordy!"

When she asked who was after him, Faulkner shouted, "The Jerries! Can't you see them?" He hit the sheets as the imaginary bullets pinged around him. "Here they come again! They're after me! They're trying to shoot me out of the sky. The goddamn Jerries, they're out to kill me. Oh, merciful Jesus!"

Within the hour, Faulkner was heading for the hospital in yet another attempt to dry out.

---

Faulkner was notorious for his heavy drinking. Once, he passed out in his bathroom at the Algonquin Hotel in New York. He was found against the radiator, his back so seared from the heat that he needed skin grafts.

## Raymond Chandler's Big Bender (1945)

Some writers go to great lengths to finish a work. To finish a screen-play, Raymond Chandler got tanked.

At fifty-seven, the writer's best work was behind him when he was hired by Paramount for a rush job. The studio's leading actor, Alan Ladd, had been drafted into the army, and the executives wanted to keep his profile with the public alive by releasing a movie while he was away. A script wasn't ready, but Chandler offered to write one based on his half-finished novel, *The Blue Dahlia*.

But with the date for Ladd's induction set, filming began with only part of the script written. Chandler worked fast, but as the filming caught up, the executives worried whether he could finish on time. With only two weeks left, a Paramount executive called Chandler and offered him a $5,000 bonus if he succeeded.

The next day, a shaken Chandler met with the producer, John Houseman. The offer, he said, implied they had no faith in him. It was an insult to his honor to take a bonus for a job he had agreed to do. Now, he didn't think he could finish the script except under one condition: He would have to get drunk. He always wrote faster that way.

Chandler had a list of his needs: two limousines with drivers available around the clock to fetch a doctor, deliver script pages to the studio, and drive the maid to market; secretaries to take dicta-tion; and a direct phone line to Houseman.

Houseman considered the risks. Chandler had been a heavy drinker most of his life before drying out. A relapse could kill him. Still, the movie had to be made, and he didn't have any alternative. He agreed, and at a celebratory lunch, Chandler loaded up with three double martinis and three double stingers.

For eight days, Chandler drank, passed out, wrote, drank, and passed out again. Twice a day, the doctor shot him up with vitamins and fed him glucose intravenously. Chandler finished the job with days to spare but spent the next month recuperating in bed.

The script's last line was "Did somebody say something about a drink of bourbon?"

## Hemingway: Like Father, Like Son (1955)

When Jack Hemingway visited his father's home outside Havana, they did what any father and son would do: drink heavily, kill buzzards, and cry over Ingrid Bergman.

They began their day at eleven by climbing the stairs to the roof of the tower where Hemingway wrote. Hemingway enjoyed potting the buzzards there, sometimes pretending they were people he didn't like, such as literary critic Bernard DeVoto or William Faulkner, who he called "Old Corndrinking Mellifluous."

The roof was baited with meat. Using high-powered shotguns, helped along by three pitchers of martinis, they blazed away, pretending that the birds were enemy planes and shouting things like, "Twelve o'clock high!" They drank away the afternoon as the carcasses plummeted around them, and by the time Papa growled "cease-fire," father and son were tanked and laughing hysterically.

The fun continued inside when Hemingway told the servant to set up the projector to screen his favorite movie, *Casablanca*. As the movie unspooled, the Hemingways talked about Ingrid Bergman in dialogue that he could have written:

"Isn't the Swede beautiful?" Ernest said. "I mean truly, really beautiful . . . beautiful."

"Yeah, Papa, beautiful. She's really, truly, truly beautiful."

The sight of Bergman's truly beautiful face reduced them to tears.

For the rest of his life, Jack remembered that afternoon as the closest he had ever been with his father.

## Behan's Tanked TV Interview (1956)

When playwright Brendan Behan's *Quare Fellow* opened at Stratford, it looked as if the play would never reach the London stage. The city's theater managers had little stomach for a grim play about an Irish prisoner that included a gay man. Then Malcolm Muggeridge invited Behan to appear on the BBC's *Panorama* talk show.

The interview looked to be another earnest, slightly dull segment, but the show's producers hadn't counted on the Irish playwright coming to the studio stewed to the gills. In the green room, he took advantage of the drinks table, singing and shouting obscenities as if he were in his favorite pub. The BBC officials considered canceling the interview, but Muggeridge pleaded with them to relent. They agreed, but he was warned: "If he uses the word cunt, don't laugh."

When Behan appeared before the cameras, he kicked off his shoes and announced he needed to take a leak. After that, he was barely coherent, so tanked that, if the producer hadn't propped him up from off-camera, he would have slid off his chair. He could have run through George Carlin's seven words you can't say on television and no one would have understood him.

"I put my first question and, allowing Behan to mumble a little, answered it myself," Muggeridge recalled with classic British understatement. "All television interviews are really like this. Behan's was simply an extreme case."

The mumble-fest ended with the playwright, at Muggeridge's request, singing a song from *The Quare Fellow* in his thin, reedy voice.

England fell in love with Behan. The next day, a man stopped him on the street and said he had understood every word he said

## The Drinks Are on Them

Here are some of your favorite writers' favorite tipples:

- Henry Fielding (1707–1754) drank champagne or ale, sometimes while chewing tobacco.
- Alfred, Lord Tennyson (1809–1892) preferred at least a bottle of port at dinner, though near the end of his life, he grumbled having to forego it for whisky.
- Oscar Wilde (1854–1900) loved wine, and absinthe for the color, saying, "What difference is there between a glass of absinthe and a sunset?"
- F. Scott Fitzgerald (1896–1940) liked champagne or gin, but when he was trying to cut back would limit himself to thirty bottles of beer. A day.
- Malcolm Lowry (1909–1957) drank everything from gin to mescal and, if nothing else was around, shaving lotion, mouthwash, and formaldehyde.
- Anne Sexton (1928–1974) carried martinis in her thermos while on the road, but otherwise preferred stingers (brandy and crème de menthe).
- Jean Rhys (1890–1979) liked whisky, Pernod, and wine, writing "one day drunk, two days hung-over, regular as clockwork."

but hadn't a clue what "that bugger Muggeridge was on about." Best of all, five London theater managers called about *The Quare Fellow*.

---

The man who declared himself "a drinker with a writing problem" was given six kegs of Guinness in return for a slogan for the company. When he came up with "Guinness Makes You Drunk," they decided to keep using "Guinness Is Good for You," coined by ad writer and mystery writer Dorothy L. Sayers.

# 19

# The End

The Grim Reaper harvests one last story.

## John Milton Rises from the Grave (1790)

It started with the best of intentions. The church of St. Giles in London was undergoing renovations, and planned to erect a memorial over the grave of John Milton, the author of *Paradise Lost*, who had died 126 years before. To make sure it was properly situated, workmen removed the church floor, uncovered a coffin that they suspected housed his remains, then called it a day.

But, while drinking at a nearby pub, someone asked how they knew Milton was inside. After all, there was no plaque on the coffin, and church records were notoriously inaccurate. They probably drank on that thought for a while, until someone said something like, "Perhaps we should find out."

The next day, an apprentice coffin maker climbed into the grave and pried back the casket's corroded lead top. Ripping open the coarse-linen shroud revealed a skeleton, gender unknown, but with long hair, similar to the poet's, that had been carefully combed and tied.

Then temptation reared its head. The workmen fell upon the bones for souvenirs. One man took a stone to Milton's upper teeth, while another considered the leg bones and lower jaw before settling for the hair.

After they left, gravedigger Elizabeth Grant took over. She hired men to collect admission and watch the windows to make sure no one got in without paying. Dragging the coffin under a pew, she sold peeks at the bones for whatever the market would bear, usually sixpence. Only when the spectators had their fill was Milton reburied.

News of Milton's involuntary resurrection and dismemberment horrified London. One church member bought back most of the remains and reburied them. But that wasn't the end for poor Milton. Rumors spread that it wasn't Milton in the coffin but a woman. Apparently, the rumormongers were ignorant that at Cambridge, he was nicknamed "the lady" for his fair complexion and effeminate nature. Nevertheless, Milton was dug up a second time so a surgeon could pronounce the bones to be masculine. Only then was Milton, at last, allowed to rest.

## Cooking Shelley (1822)

On an isolated, windswept beach near Viareggio, Italy, a grim group of men climbed out of boats and waded toward the shore. The party of two Englishmen, an Italian health official, and several soldiers had an unpleasant task ahead.

They were there to cremate a poet.

Five weeks before, Percy Bysshe Shelley drowned during a

storm in his schooner along with his friend Edward Williams and a boy. Their bodies washed up on shore a week later, where they were buried until arrangements could be made for a cremation.

Shelley's friend Edward Trelawny organized the expedition. A grill of iron bars and sheet-iron supported on a stand was built. Workmen were hired. Lord Byron, who lived nearby, was invited to attend. Shelley's widow, Mary, was not.

The party found Williams's body, exhumed it, and spent the rest of the afternoon burning it. The next day, it was Shelley's turn. As they cleared away the sand, they saw a ghastly sight. Fish had stripped the flesh from Shelley's face and hands, revealing bone and tendon. Trelawny had to identify his friend by the copy of Aeschylus found in one pocket, and Keats's poems in the other, doubled back, "as if the reader, in the act of reading, had hastily thrust it away."

Byron asked for the skull, but Trelawney said no. He knew the last skull Byron got ahold of was made into a drinking cup.

Shelley was laid on the grill and the driftwood set alight. Trelawney noted how "more wine was poured over Shelley's dead body than he had consumed during his life. This with the oil and salt made the yellow flames glisten and quiver. . . . The corpse fell open and the heart was laid bare. The frontal bone of the skull, where it had been struck with the mattock, fell off; and, as the back of the head rested on the red-hot bottom bars of the furnace, the brains literally seethed, bubbled and boiled as in a cauldron."

All that was left of the poet were bone fragments, the jaw and skull and his heart. Trelawney snatched the heart off the pyre and gave it to Mary, who kept it the rest of her life.

**Shelley's death was not universally mourned in England. One newspaper, remembering his atheism, announced: "Shelley, the writer of some infidel poetry, has been drowned, *now* he knows whether there is a God or no."**

## Rossetti Robs a Grave (1869)

When Elizabeth Siddal died of laudanum poisoning at thirty-two, painter Dante Gabriel Rossetti was bereft at the loss of his wife, model, and muse. He was so distraught that before her casket was closed, he placed close to her lips and intertwined in her long, coppery golden hair a small calf-bound journal containing the sole copy of his poems.

Seven years later, when he decided to publish a volume of his poetry, he realized that he had interred his most important works with his wife.

To get them back, he used his connections with the Home Office to have the coffin exhumed, and entrusted the task to Charles Augustus Howell, a London dandy with flexible ethics. Desecrating his wife's grave to recover his poems would have looked bad, so secrecy was vital. To ensure Howell's silence, Rossetti promised "I will give you the swellest drawing conceivable."

When permission was granted, Rossetti stayed home while, in the middle of the night, Howell accompanied the doctors and gravediggers to the cemetery and dug up Elizabeth.

Rossetti was pleased with what they found. "All in the coffin was found quite perfect," he wrote his brother, "but the book, though not in any way destroyed, is soaked through and through and had to be still further saturated with disinfectants."

The poems were published to great acclaim, but the exhumation troubled Rossetti the rest of his life. "I suppose the truth must ooze out in time," Rossetti wrote, and he was right. Eight years after Rossetti died, Howell was found dead in mysterious circumstances—in a ditch outside a pub, with his throat slashed and a ten-shilling piece lodged between his teeth—and Rossetti's letters containing his secret were found among Howell's papers.

## Chekhov's Last Act (1904)

As a dramatist, Anton Chekhov would have appreciated his death scene if he weren't so busy dying. Like his plays, such as *The Cherry Orchard*, it was tragic, poetic, and even a little farcical.

Chekhov's final act opened at a German spa, where, at forty-four, he sought treatment for tuberculosis. While he hoped for a cure, he knew from his medical training the true state of his health. Before leaving Russia, he confided to a friend, "I am going away to croak."

He was allowed outdoors, but most of his time was spent in bed, coughing and feverish. His wife, Olga, was taught to inject him with morphine and digitalis and to administer oxygen. He dreamed of writing a play about passengers on an icebound ship. Mostly, though, he was bored.

On his last day, Chekhov awoke at 2 a.m., muttering that his sailor nephew Kolia was in danger. Olga administered chloral hydrate and placed ice over his heart. The doctor came, checked his patient's pulse, and then—customary then for dying patients—called for champagne. A doctor himself, Chekhov knew what that meant. He sat up and shouted, "I am dying."

The bottle came. Chekhov polished off a glass, murmured, "I haven't had champagne for a long time," and died.

In the morning, to protect the spa's guests, a laundry basket was brought to help move the playwright. But rigor mortis made it difficult to hide the body. The best they could do was bend Chekhov into a half-sitting position and cover him with a sheet.

"I walked behind the men carrying the body," a witness wrote. "Light and shade from the burning torches flickered and leaped over the dead man's face, and at times it seemed to me as if Chekhov was scarcely perceptibly smiling at the fact that, by decreeing that his body should be carried in a laundry basket, Fate had linked him with humour even in death."

> Chekhov's funeral was anything but serious. The procession to the graveyard crossed paths with the funeral cortège of a Russian general, and some mourners ended up following the wrong body. At the cemetery, onlookers hung from trees and clambered atop the monuments, commenting on the bereaved family as if it were a spectator sport. "This is how we treat our great writers," author Maxim Gorky fumed.

## Malcolm Lowry's Mysterious Death (1957)

One of literature's great drunks, British writer Malcolm Lowry left behind broken promises, broken bottles, and broken works. He wrote copiously, but published only two books; one of which, *Under the Volcano*, is considered one of the great novels of the twentieth century.

As much as he loved writing, he loved drinking more, and Lowry was violent when he was drunk. His behavior in Mexico, where he had set and written most of *Volcano*, led to divorce, multiple mental breakdowns, and his flight to the United States. There, he married Margerie Bonner and moved to Canada. They settled in a squatter's shack on the coast outside Vancouver. There, in isolated splendor, Lowry found his Eden and was able to finish *Volcano*.

But when the shack—built without permission—was demolished, he and Bonner decided to rent a cottage in East Sussex, England. He tried to stay sober, using aversion therapy and hospitalization, but Bonner's drinking and his addiction were too strong. The more he drank, the more his health faltered and he found it harder to write. Worse, he suspected that Bonner was cheating on him.

The unhappy couple spent the last night of his life drinking. During the inevitable argument, Bonner smashed the gin bottle, and Lowry threatened her with the shards. She fled to a neighbor's house to spend the night. The next morning, she returned, and amid the glass, splintered furniture, and scattered food, she found Lowry on the bedroom floor, dead.

The coroner declared the cause of death as "misadventure" from an overdose of sleeping pills. But as Bonner told her story to police and friends, inconsistencies cropped up. She told friends—but not police—that she had destroyed a suicide note. She was seen with a bottle of sleeping pills that turned up, empty, in a drawer in the spare bedroom. Lowry's friends were suspicious. The thought of a drunken Lowry with the shakes twisting off the cap on a pill bottle, replacing it, then hiding the bottle in the next room, seemed unbelievable.

The truth behind Lowry's death will never be known, but he may have had a premonition of his fatal destiny: he had told a psychiatrist that either he was going to kill Bonner or she was going to kill him.

## Mishima's Last Act (1970)

For more than twenty years, Yukio Mishima towered over Japanese art and literature, producing a flood of novels, poems, essays, and plays in the classical Noh and Kabuki styles. Considered by many one of the country's most important novelists, he was nominated for the Nobel Prize for literature three times.

Mishima was also a mess of contradictions. He praised Japanese traditions and criticized Western decadence, but embraced the West's literature, lifestyles, and arts. He was an intellectual who yearned to be a man of action and sculpted his body through martial arts and bodybuilding. He was homosexual, yet married and fathered children. In short, he was as macho as Norman Mailer but as homoerotic as the young Truman Capote.

But Mishima yearned most for Japan to return to its imperialistic past. To this end, he formed the Shield Society, a private army dedicated to inspiring the return of Bushido, the samurai code of honor. To succeed in this, he was willing to risk everything, even his life.

So on November 25, Mishima and three supporters entered the Ichigaya Camp in Tokyo. He met with the commander—who knew Mishima—then overpowered him and held him hostage. The camp's soldiers were ordered to assemble in formation outside the commander's window, and Mishima, in his Shield Society uniform, harangued them. He denounced the decadence that Japan had fallen into and urged them to revolt and save the country by returning it to its former glory.

The soldiers, remembering how well that worked the last time, weren't having any of it. They heckled and mocked Mishima. Considering his duty done, he returned to the office, where he removed his jacket and bared his chest. Kneeling, he took an ancient samurai dagger, plunged it into his belly, and disemboweled himself. An assistant cut off his head. It took three tries.

In death, Mishima set an example for all writers to follow. Not to kill yourself after being humiliated—although that would make the National Book Awards watchable—but to always meet your

# Writers' Colonies of the Dead

Like real estate, the most important factor in a writer's final resting ground is location, location, location. Writers and literary fans looking for a tomb with a view should check out these neighborhoods:

- Kensel Green, London: Established 1837. For admirers of classic English literature. Home to William Makepeace Thackeray, Wilkie Collins, poet Leigh Hunt, and Anthony Trollope.
- Sleepy Hollow Cemetery, Concord, Massachusetts: The American equivalent to Kensel Green, where Louisa May Alcott, Ralph Waldo Emerson, Nathaniel Hawthorne, and Henry David Thoreau hang their hats.
- Forest Lawn, Glendale, California: While better known as the movie stars' final resting place, there are plenty of tourists willing to make a side trip to visit L. Frank Baum, Clifford Odets, Louis L'Amour, and Theodore Dreiser.
- Le Pere Lachaise: A sure sign you've arrived. More than eight hundred thousand come here yearly to visit the million or so Frenchmen, laid alongside an international cast of writers: Oscar Wilde, Richard Wright, Molière, Balzac, Gertrude Stein, and Marcel Proust.

deadlines. Before he set out on his suicide mission, Mishima made sure to turn in the last pages of his final novel.

> Mishima's macho behavior might have been compensation for what he considered an act of cowardice. When he was drafted near the end of World War II, Mishima faked tuberculosis to get out of serving.

# Acknowledgments

This book could not have been written without the generous help and valuable advice of these people and institutions: my agent, Rita Rosenkranz, who steered the project in the right direction; my editor, Meg Leder (assisted by intern Brian Sweeney), who supplied notes, suggestions, and reputation-saving corrections; my publicist, Caitlin Mulrooney-Lyski; the staff of the Hershey Public Library, particularly Denise Phillips, who probably wondered why I needed all these books but cheerfully provided them anyway; the staff of the Dauphin County Public Library, who performed the same service; the newspapers and magazines that supplied much of the material, including the *New York Times*, *Washington Post*, *London Times*, *Daily Telegraph*, *Guardian*, *New York*, and *Esquire*; Jonathan Maberry; Pennwriters; Google Books; iTunes; and, again, my wife, Teresa. Your faith, encouragement, and advice mean more to me than I can express.

Last but not least, thank you to all the writers whose feuds, frolics, and follies contributed to the making of this book, and to the rest of you—calm, productive, and not at all insane—who inspired, educated, and advised me.

# Bibliography

## HORATIO ALGER

John A. Geck, "Biographies: The Lives of Horatio Alger Jr.," *The Novels of Horatio Alger Jr.*, available at www.lib.rochester.edu/camelot/cinder/bio.htm, accessed October 20, 2009.

Jack Bales Scharnhorst, *The Lost Life of Horatio Alger Jr.*, Bloomington: Indiana University Press, 1985.

## NELSON ALGREN

Joan Acocella, *Twenty-Eight Artists and Two Saints*, New York: Pantheon, 2007.

Bettina Drew, *Nelson Algren: A Life on the Wild Side*, New York: G. P. Putnam's Sons, 1989.

## KINGSLEY AMIS

Zachary Leader, *The Life of Kingsley Amis*, New York: Pantheon, 2006.

## MARTIN AMIS

Martin Amis, *Experience: A Memoir*, New York: Vintage, 2001.

## HANS CHRISTIAN ANDERSEN

Dalya Alberge, "Hans Christian Andersen's Visit Was No Fairytale for Dickens," *Times*, May 26, 2008, available at http://entertainment.timesonline.co.uk/tol/arts_and_entertainment/books/article4004516.ece, accessed September 22, 2009.

"A Visit to Charles Dickens by Hans Christian Andersen," *Bentley's Miscellany*, vol. 48, Bentley, 1860.

Elias Bredsdorff, *Hans Christian Andersen: The Story of His Life and Work 1805–1875*, London: Phaidon Press, 1975.

## MAXWELL ANDERSON

Hesper Anderson, *South Mountain Road: A Daughter's Journey of Discovery*, New York: Simon & Schuster, 2000.

Mel Gussow, "Stage View: When Writers Turn the Tables Rather Than the Other Cheek," *New York Times*, July 16, 1989, available at www.nytimes .com/1989/07/16/theater/stage-view-when-writers-turn-the-tables-rather-than -the-other-cheek.html, accessed November 3, 2009.

"The Theater: Café Brawl," *Time*, March 11, 1946, available at www.time.com/time/ magazine/article/0,9171,776737,00.html, accessed November 3, 2009.


## SHERWOOD ANDERSON

Kim Townsend, *Sherwood Anderson*, Boston: Houghton Mifflin, 1987.


## PIERS ANTHONY

Piers Anthony, *But What of Earth?* New York: Tor, 1989.


## JOHN JAMES AUDUBON

Richard Rhodes, *John James Audubon: The Making of an American*, New York: Knopf, 2004.


## HONORÉ DE BALZAC

Graham Robb, *Balzac*, New York: W.W. Norton & Company, 1996.


## CHARLES BAUDELAIRE

Joanna Richardson, *Baudelaire*, New York: St. Martin's Press, 1994.


## SAMUEL BECKETT

Deirdre Bair, *Samuel Beckett: A Biography*, New York: Simon & Schuster, 1990.

Samuel Beckett, et al., *Beckett Remembering, Remembering Beckett: A Centenary Celebration*, New York: Arcade Publishing, 2006.

Mary V. Dearborn, *Mistress of Modernism: The Life of Peggy Guggenheim*, Boston: Houghton Mifflin Harcourt, 2004.

James Knowlson, *Damned to Fame: The Life of Samuel Beckett*, New York: Grove Press, 2004.

Benjamin Kunkel, "Sam I Am," *New Yorker*, June 7, 2006.

## BRENDAN BEHAN

J. P. Donleavy, *The History of the Ginger Man*, Boston: Houghton Mifflin, 1994.
Malcolm Muggeridge, "Brendan Behan at Lime Grove," *New Statesman*, March 27, 1964, available at www.newstatesman.com/199912060031, accessed July 14, 2009.
Scott Murray, "Joy of Six: Broadcasting Under the Influence," *Guardian*, June 16, 2009.

## HILAIRE BELLOC

A. N. Wilson, *Hilaire Belloc*, New York: Atheneum, 1984.

## JAMES BOSWELL

Rick Allen, *The Moving Pageant: A Literary Sourcebook on London Street-Life, 1700–1914*, London: Routledge, 1998.
Vic Gatrell, *City of Laughter: Sex and Satire in Eighteenth-Century*, New York: Walker & Co., 2006.

## EMILY BRONTË

Juliet Barker, "Brontë, Emily Jane (1818–1848)," *Oxford Dictionary of National Biography*. Oxford University Press, 2004, available at www.oxforddnb.com/view/article/3524, accessed October 24, 2004.
David W. Harrison, *The Brontës of Haworth*, Victoria, BC: Trafford, 2003.

## PEARL S. BUCK

Peter Conn, *Pearl S. Buck: A Cultural Biography*, Cambridge: Cambridge University Press, 1998.

## WILLIAM F. BUCKLEY JR.

Harry Kloman, "Political Animals: Vidal, Buckley and the '68 Conventions," available at www.pitt.edu/~kloman/debates.html, accessed September 3, 2009.
"On Mr. Buckley and Civility," *The Rush Limbaugh Show*, February 28, 2008, available at www.rushlimbaugh.com/home/daily/site_022808/content/01125106.guest.html, accessed July 10, 2009.

## ANTHONY BURGESS

Roger Lewis, *Anthony Burgess*, New York: St. Martin's Press, 2002.

**ROBERT BURNS**

Richard Hindle Fowler, *Robert Burns*, London: Routledge, 1988.

H.C.G. Matthew and Brian Harrison, *Dictionary of National Biography*, New York: Oxford University Press, 2004.

*Poems, Songs and Letters: Being the Complete Works of Robert Burns*, Macmillan, 1893.


**WILLIAM S. BURROUGHS**

James Campbell, *This Is the Beat Generation*, London: Martin Secker & Warburg, 1999.

Edward de Grazia, *Girls Lean Back Everywhere: The Law of Obscenity and the Assault on Genius*, New York: Vintage, 1993.

Richard Severo, "William S. Burroughs Dies at 83," *New York Times*, August 3, 1997.


**LORD BYRON**

John Keats Forum, available at www.john-keats.com/phpboard/viewtopic .php?f=2&t=356, accessed August 13, 2009.

Susan J. Wolfson, *The Cambridge Companion to Keats*, Cambridge: Cambridge University Press, 2001.


**JAMES BRANCH CABELL**

"Jurgen, A Comedy of Justice," Wikipedia, available at http://en.wikipedia.org/wiki/ Jurgen,_A_Comedy_of_Justice, accessed September 2, 2009.

"Jurgen Is Proper, Judge Nott Rules," *New York Times*, October 20, 1922.

Mary Alice Kirkpatrick, "Summary of Jurgen: A Comedy of Justice," *Library of Southern Literature*, available at http://docsouth.unc.edu/southlit/cabell1/summary.html, accessed September 2, 2009.

"Under the Censor's Axe," *New York Times*, September 26, 1920.


**TRUMAN CAPOTE**

Gerald Clarke, *Capote: A Biography*, New York: Carroll & Graf, 1988.


**RAYMOND CHANDLER**

Raymond Chandler, *The Blue Dahlia: A Screenplay*, Carbondale: Southern Illinois University Press, 1976.

Judith Freeman, *The Long Embrace*, New York: Pantheon, 2007.

Tom Hiney, *Raymond Chandler: A Biography*, New York: Atlantic Monthly Press, 1997.

## ANTON CHEKHOV

Julian Evans, "Chekhov's Last Hours," *Daily Telegraph*, July 4, 2004, available at www.telcgraph.co.uk/culture/books/3620039/Chekhovs-last-hours.html, accessed June 26, 2009.

Donald Rayfield, *Anton Chekhov: A Life*, New York: Henry Holt, 1998.

## AGATHA CHRISTIE

Jared Cade, *Agatha Christie and the Eleven Missing Days*, London: Peter Owen, 2006.

Agatha Christie, *Agatha Christie: An Autobiography*, New York: Dodd, Mead, 1977.

Janet Morgan, *Agatha Christie: A Biography*, New York: HarperCollins, 1986.

## COLLEY CIBBER

Helene Koon, *Colley Cibber*, Lexington: University Press of Kentucky, 1982.

## SAMUEL TAYLOR COLERIDGE

John Barrell, "Inside the Head," *London Review of Books*, November 2, 2000.

John Beer, "Coleridge, Samuel Taylor (1772–1834)," *Oxford Dictionary of National Biography*, Oxford University Press, 2004, available at www.oxforddnb.com/view/article/5888, accessed October 25, 2004.

Philip Gooden, *The Mammoth Book of Literary Anecdotes*, New York: Carroll & Graf, 2002.

Nicholas Roe, *Samuel Taylor Coleridge and the Sciences of Life*, New York: Oxford University Press, 2002.

## COLETTE

"Colette," Wikipedia, available at http://en.wikipedia.org/wiki/Colette, accessed September 11, 2009.

Christopher Petkanas, "Belles Lettres," *New York Times*, August 16, 2009, available at www.nytimes.com/2009/08/16/style/tmagazine/16colette.html, accessed September 3, 2009.

## JOSEPH CONRAD

Zdzislaw Najder, *Joseph Conrad: A Life*, Rochester, NY: Camden House, 2007.

## NOËL COWARD

Noël Coward and Barry Day, *The Letters of Noël Coward*, New York: Knopf, 2007.

## STEPHEN CRANE

Christopher Benfey, *The Double Life of Stephen Crane*, New York: Knopf, 1992.
Mark Sufrin, *Stephen Crane*, New York: Atheneum, 1992.


## SIMONE DE BEAUVOIR

Joan Acocella, *Twenty-Eight Artists and Two Saints*, New York: Pantheon, 2007.
Bettina Drew, *Nelson Algren: A Life on the Wild Side*, New York: G. P. Putnam's Sons,
    1989.


## DANIEL DEFOE

Wilfred Whitten, *Daniel Defoe*, Small, Maynard, 1800.


## PHILIP K. DICK

Philip K. Dick and Gregg Rickman, *Philip K. Dick: The Last Testament*, Long Beach,
    CA: Fragments West/The Valentine Press, 1985.
Lawrence Sutin, *Divine Invasions: A Life of Philip K. Dick*, New York: Harmony, 1989.


## CHARLES DICKENS

Dalya Alberge, "Hans Christian Andersen's Visit Was No Fairytale for Dickens,"
    *Times*, May 26, 2008, available at http://entertainment.timesonline.co.uk/
    tol/arts_and_entertainment/books/article4004516.ece, accessed September 22,
    2009.
"A Visit to Charles Dickens by Hans Christian Andersen," *Bentley's Miscellany*, vol.
    48, Bentley, 1860.
Elias Bredsdorff, *Hans Christian Andersen: The Story of His Life and Work 1805–1875*,
    London: Phaidon Press, 1975.
R. Shelton Mackenzie, *Life of Charles Dickens*, Peterson & Brothers, 1870.


## J. P. DONLEAVY

J. P. Donleavy, *The History of the Ginger Man*, Boston: Houghton Mifflin, 1994.


## JOHN DONNE

John Donne and Paul M. Oliver, *Selected Letters*, London: Routledge, 2002.
Augustus Jessopp, *John Donne, Sometime Dean of St. Paul's*, London: Methuen, 1897.
"John Donne," LoveToKnow 1911, available at www.1911encyclopedia.org/John_
    Donne, accessed June 1, 2010.

## FYODOR DOSTOYEVSKY

Joseph Frank, *Dostoevsky: The Years of Ordeal, 1850–1859*, Princeton: Princeton University Press, 1987.

Peter Sekirin, *The Dostoevsky Archive: Firsthand Accounts of the Novelist from Contemporary Memoirs and Rare Periodicals*, Jefferson, NC: McFarland, 1997.


## THEODORE DREISER

Sherwood Anderson, *Sherwood Anderson's Memoirs*, Chapel Hill: University of North Carolina Press, 1969.

Gerald Clarke, "Publishing Was His Line," *Time*, August 22, 1977, available at www .time.com/time/magazine/article/0,9171,915321-2,00.html, accessed September 15, 2009.

Robert Hendrickson, *American Literary Anecdotes*, New York: Facts on File, 1990.

James R. Mellow, *Invented Lives: F. Scott and Zelda Fitzgerald*, Boston: Houghton, Mifflin, 1984.


## JOHN DRYDEN

Graham Greene, *Lord Rochester's Monkey*, New York: Penguin, 1976.

H.C.G. Matthew and Brian Harrison, *Dictionary of National Biography*, New York: Oxford University Press, 2004.


## MARGUERITE DURAS

Laure Adler and Anne-Marie Glasheen, *Marguerite Duras: A Life*, Chicago: University of Chicago Press, 2000.

Ronald Tiersky, *François Mitterrand: A Very French President*, Lanham, MD: Bowman & Littlefield, 2002.


## WILLIAM FAULKNER

Peter Applebome, "New Focus on Faulkner as True Man of Letters," *New York Times*, July 6, 1989.

Tom Dardis, *The Thirsty Muse*, Boston: Houghton Mifflin, 1989.

Jay Parini, "William Faulkner: 'Not an Educated Man,'" *Chronicle*, November 26, 2004, available at http://chronicle.com/free/v51/i14/14b00601.htm, accessed May 6, 2008.


## F. SCOTT FITZGERALD

The Baltimore Literary Heritage Project, "So We Beat on, Boats Against the Current," available at http://baltimoreauthors.ubalt.edu/writers/fscottfitzgerald.htm, accessed July 9, 2009.

Matthew Bruccoli and Scottie Fitzgerald Smith, *Some Sort of Epic Grandeur*, New York: Harcourt, 1981.

Tom Dardis, *The Thirsty Muse*, Boston: Houghton Mifflin, 1989.

R.W.B. Lewis, "Edith Wharton: The Beckoning Quarry," available at www .americanheritage.com/articles/magazine/ah/1975/6/1975_6_52.shtml, accessed September 10, 2009.

R.W.B. Lewis and Nancy Lewis, *The Letters of Edith Wharton*, New York: Scribner, 1988.

Marion Mainwaring, *Mysteries of Paris: The Quest for Morton Fullerton*, Hanover, NH: University Press of New England, 2001.

Jeffrey Meyers, *Scott Fitzgerald*, New York: HarperCollins, 1994.

"Show Business: Giant Killer," *Time*, February 29, 1960, available at www.time.com/ time/magazine/article/0,9171,873264,00.html, accessed July 9, 2009.

Andrew Turnbull, *Scott Fitzgerald*, London: Bodley Head, 1962.


## GUSTAVE FLAUBERT

Edmond de Goncourt and Jules de Goncourt, *Pages from the Goncourt Journals*, New York: New York Review of Books Classics, 2006.


## FREDERICK FORSYTH

"Author Stumbles on G-Bissau Drama," available at http://news.bbc.co.uk/2/hi/ 7921847.stm, accessed October 26, 2009.

Maurice Chittenden, "Forsyth: My Real-life Dogs of War Coup," *Sunday Times*, June 11, 2006, available at www.timesonline.co.uk/tol/news/uk/article673684.ece, accessed October 25, 2009.


## JANET FRAME

Michael King, *Wrestling with the Angel: A Life of Janet Frame*, New York: Counterpoint Press, 2000.

New Zealand Book Council, "Janet Frame," available at www.bookcouncil.org.nz/ writers/framej.html, accessed October 6, 2009.


## ROBERT FROST

Wallace Stegner, *The Uneasy Chair: A Biography of Bernard DeVoto*, Lincoln, NE: Bison Books, 2001.


## MARTHA GELLHORN

Eamonn Fitzgerald, "The Anniversary of Martha Gellhorn's D-Day," available at www.spotlight-online.de/blogs/eamonn-fitzgerald/the-anniversary-of-martha -gellhorns-d-day, accessed July 9, 2009.

Caroline Moorehead, *Gellhorn: A Twentieth-Century Life*, New York: Henry Holt, 2003.


## CHARLOTTE PERKINS GILMAN
Cynthia J. Davis, *Charlotte Perkins Gilman*, Stanford: Stanford University Press, 2010.


## ALLEN GINSBERG
Allen Ginsberg and Louis Ginsberg, *Family Business: Selected Letters Between a Father and Son*, New York: Bloomsbury, 2001.
"Howl," Wikipedia, available at http://en.wikipedia.org/wiki/Howl, accessed October 20, 2009.
"John Burroughs and Allen Ginsberg Are 'Practically Related,'" *Choriamb*, November 2, 2004, available at http://choriamb.wordpress.com/2004/11/02/john-burroughs -and-allen-ginsberg-are-practically-related, accessed June 1, 2010.
Jonah Raskin, *American Scream: Allen Ginsberg's Howl and the Making of the Beat Generation*, Berkeley and Los Angeles: University of California Press, 2006.


## JOHANN GOETHE
Joseph-Francois Angelloz, *Goethe*, New York: Orion Press, 1958.
Benedikt Wahler, "The Sorrows of Young Werther," available at www.benwahler.net/ WerthersWelt/werthere.htm, accessed July 9, 2009.


## WILLIAM GOLDING
Richard Brooks, "Author William Golding Tried to Rape Girl, 15," *Sunday Times*, August 16, 2009, available at http://entertainment.timesonline.co.uk/tol/arts_ and_entertainment/books/article6797774.ece, accessed August 18, 2009.
Blake Morrison, "William Golding by John Carey," *Guardian*, September 5, 2009, available at www.guardian.co.uk/books/2009/sep/05/william-golding-john -carey-review, accessed October 20, 2009.


## OLIVIA GOLDSMITH
Ralph Gardner Jr., "Looks to Die For," *New York*, February 9, 2004.
Aileen Jacobson, "A Tragic Ending," *Newsday*, February 10, 2004.


## GRAHAM GREENE
Richard Greene, *Graham Greene: A Life in Letters*, New York: W.W. Norton & Company, 2008.

234 *Bibliography*

**RADCLYFFE HALL**

Edward de Grazia, *Girls Lean Back Everywhere: The Law of Obscenity and the Assault on Genius*, New York: Vintage, 1993.
Katie Roiphe, *Uncommon Arrangements*, New York: Random House, 2008.

**DASHIELL HAMMETT**

Dashiell Hammett, Richard Layman, and Julie M. Rivett, *Selected Letters of Dashiell Hammett: 1921–1960*, New York: Counterpoint, 2001.
Joan Mellen, *Hellman and Hammett: The Legendary Passion of Lillian Hellman and Dashiell Hammett*, New York: HarperCollins, 1996.

**LILLIAN HELLMAN**

Carol Brightman, *Writing Dangerously: Mary McCarthy and Her World*, New York: Clarkson Potter, 1992.

**ERNEST HEMINGWAY**

Carlos Baker, *Ernest Hemingway: A Life Story*, New York: Scribner, 1969.
Jackson J. Benson, *The True Adventures of John Steinbeck, Writer*, New York: Viking, 1984.
Tom Dardis, *The Thirsty Muse*, Boston: Houghton Mifflin, 1989.
Gioia Diliberto, *Hadley*, New York: Ticknor & Fields, 1992.
Ernest Hemingway and Carlos Baker, *Ernest Hemingway Selected Letters 1917–1961*, New York: Scribner. 2003.
A. E. Hotchner, *Papa Hemingway: A Personal Memoir*, New York: Da Capo Press, 2005.
Jeffrey Meyers, *Hemingway: A Biography*, New York: Da Capo Press, 1999.

**O. HENRY**

Walter Hines Page, *The World's Work, vol. 33: Nov. 1916 to April 1917*, Garden City, NY: Doubleday, Page & Co., 1916–1917.

**PATRICIA HIGHSMITH**

Andrew Wilson, *Beautiful Shadow: A Life of Patricia Highsmith*, London: Bloomsbury, 2004.

**TED HUGHES**

Sylvia Plath and Karen V. Kukil, *The Unabridged Journals of Sylvia Plath, 1950–1962*, New York: Random House, 2000.

Obituary: Ted Hughes, *Daily Telegraph*, October 30, 1998, available at www.telegraph
.co.uk/news/obituaries/5886550/Ted-Hughes.html, accessed June 1, 2010.


## VICTOR HUGO

Madame Duclaux, *Victor Hugo*, London: Constable, 1921.

Graham Robb, *Victor Hugo: A Biography*, New York: W.W. Norton & Company, 1999.


## DAVID HUME

David Edmonds and John Eidinow, *Rousseau's Dog: Two Great Thinkers at War in the
Age of Enlightenment*, New York: Ecco, 2006.


## CLIFFORD IRVING

Mick Brown, "You Couldn't Make It Up," *Daily Telegraph*, July 28, 2007, available at
www.telegraph.co.uk/culture/3666824/You-couldnt-make-it-up.html, accessed
August 24, 2007.

Paul Whitington, "How Howard Hughes Foiled the Great Hoax," *Independent*, July 28,
2007, available at www.independent.ie/entertainment/film-cinema/how-howard
-hughes-foiled-the-great-hoax-1046784.html, accessed September 3, 2009.


## SHIRLEY JACKSON

Brendan Gill, *Here at the New Yorker*, New York: Random House, 1975.


## ALFRED JARRY

"Alfred Jarry," Wikipedia, available at http://en.wikipedia.org/wiki/Alfred_Jarry,
accessed October 20, 2009.

Michael Largo, *Genius and Heroin*, New York: Harper, 2009.

"Ubu Roi," Wikipedia, available at http://en.wikipedia.org/wiki/Ubu_Roi, accessed
October 20, 2009.


## SAMUEL JOHNSON

F. E. Halliday, *Doctor Johnson and His World*, London: Thames and Hudson, 1968.

Christopher Hitchens, "Demons and Dictionaries," *Atlantic*, March 2009, available at
www.theatlantic.com/magazine/archive/2009/03/demons-and-dictionaries/7272,
accessed June 1, 2010.

H.C.G. Matthew, and Brian Harrison, *Dictionary of National Biography*, New York:
Oxford University Press, 2004.

## ERICA JONG
Erica Jong, *Seducing the Demon: Writing for My Life*, New York: Tarcher, 2006.


## BEN JONSON
Jesse Franklin Bradley, *The Jonson Allusion-Book: A Collection of Allusions to Ben Jonson from 1597–1700*, New Haven, CT: Yale University Press, 1897.
Rosalind Miles, *Ben Jonson: His Life and Work*, London: Routledge & Kegan Paul, 1986.


## JAMES JOYCE
A. Nicholas Fargnoli and Michael P. Gillespie, *James Joyce A–Z*, New York: Oxford University Press, 1995.


## FRANZ KAFKA
Dalya Alberge, "Franz Kafka's Porn Brought Out of the Closet," *Times*, August 2, 2008, available at http://entertainment.timesonline.co.uk/tol/arts_and_entertainment/books/article4446131.ece, accessed September 3, 2009.
James Hawes, *Why You Should Read Kafka Before You Waste Your Life*, New York: St. Martin's, 2008.


## EDWARD KYNASTON
Robert Lathan and William Matthews, eds., *The Diary of Samuel Pepys*, vol. 9, Berkeley and Los Angeles, University of California Press, 2000.


## CAROLINE LAMB
Caroline Franklin, "Lamb, Lady Caroline (1785–1828)," *Oxford Dictionary of National Biography*, Oxford University Press, 2004, available at www.oxforddnb.com/view/article/15911, accessed October 23, 2004.
Jerome McGann, "Byron, George Gordon Noel, sixth Baron Byron (1788–1824)," *Oxford Dictionary of National Biography*, Oxford University Press, 2004, available at www.oxforddnb.com/view/article/4279, accessed October 23, 2004.


## MARY LAMB
Mark Bostridge, "A Double Life: A Biography of Charles and Mary Lamb, by Sarah Burton," *Independent*, August 17, 2003. Available at http://enjoyment.independent.co.uk/books/reviews/story.jsp?story=43506, accessed August 18, 2003.

Susan Tyler Hitchcock, *Mad Mary Lamb: Lunacy and Murder in Literary London*, New York: W.W. Norton, 2005.


## SINCLAIR LEWIS
Arnold Leslie Lazarus, *The George Jean Nathan Reader*, Rutherford, NJ: Fairleigh Dickinson University Press, 1990.
Richard Lingeman, *Sinclair Lewis: Rebel from Main Street*, New York: Random House, 2002.
Mark Schorer, *Sinclair Lewis*, Minneapolis: University of Minnesota Press, 1963.


## MARIO VARGAS LLOSA
Gerald Martin, *Gabriel García Márquez: A Life*, New York: Random House, 2009.
Paul Vallely, "Best of Enemies: The Truth Behind a 30-Year Literary Feud," *Independent*, March 13, 2007, available at www.independent.co.uk/arts-entertainment/books/features/best-of-enemies-the-truth-behind-a-30year-literary-feud-440035.html, accessed September 22, 2009.


## JACK LONDON
"Jack London's Adventure in the Klondike," available at www.beyondbooks.com/LAM12/3a.asp, accessed September 24, 2009.
Jack L. McSherry III, *Arctic Website*, "Jack London's Klondike Adventure," available at www.arcticwebsite.com/LondonJackKlond.html, accessed September 24, 2009.


## ROBERT LOWELL
Carla Blumenkranz, "Deeply and Mysteriously Implicated," available at www.poetryfoundation.org/journal/article.html?id=178893, accessed December 19, 2006.
Ruth Price, *The Lives of Agnes Smedley*, New York: Oxford University Press, 2005.


## MALCOLM LOWRY
Gordon Bowker, "Lowry's Mysterious Death," *Times Literary Supplement*, February 19, 2004.


## NORMAN MAILER
Mary V. Dearborn, *Mailer: A Biography*, Boston: Houghton, Mifflin & Harcourt, 2001.

Mark Gado, "Jack Abbott: From the Belly of the Beast," available at www.trutv.com/
library/crime/notorious_murders/celebrity/jack_abbott/index.html, accessed August
24, 2009.

Malcolm Jones, "You're in the Lap of History," *Newsweek*, January 27, 2003, available
at www.newsweek.com/id/62926, accessed July 20, 2003.

Boris Kachka, "Mr. Tendentious," *New York*, available at http://nymag.com/arts/
books/features/26285, accessed February 3, 2010.

Peter Kobel, "Crime and Punishment," *Entertainment Weekly*, available at www
.ew.com/ew/article/0,,316162,00.html, accessed November 4, 2009.

Peter Manso, *Mailer: His Life and Times*, New York: Simon & Schuster, 1985.

Susan Shapiro, "Feuding Writers Get Nasty," *Village Voice Literary Supplement*, April 2000.

Dan Wakefield, *New York in the 50s*, New York: Macmillan, 1999.


## ERN MALLEY

David Lehman, "The Ern Malley Poetry Hoax," *Jacket* 17, June 17, 2002, available at
http://jacketmagazine.com/17/ern-dl.html, accessed November 5, 2009.

David Nason, "Some Australian Heroes," *Australian*, March 24, 2001.


## KATHERINE MANSFIELD

Antony Alpers, *Katherine Mansfield: A Biography*, New York: Knopf, 1954.

D. H. Lawrence, John Worthen, and Lindeth Vasey, *The First "Women in Love,"*
Cambridge: Cambridge University Press, 2002.

Katherine Mansfield, Vincent O'Sullivan, and Margaret Scott, *The Collected Letters
of Katherine Mansfield: 1903–1917*, New York: Oxford University Press, 1984.


## GABRIEL GARCÍA MÁRQUEZ

Gerald Martin, *Gabriel García Márquez: A Life*, New York: Random House, 2009.

Paul Vallely, "Best of Enemies: The Truth Behind a 30-Year Literary Feud," *Independent*,
March 13, 2007, available at www.independent.co.uk/arts-entertainment/books/
features/best-of-enemies-the-truth-behind-a-30year-literary-feud-440035.html,
accessed September 22, 2009.


## EDGAR LEE MASTERS

Matthew D. Norman, "An Illinois Iconoclast: Edgar Lee Masters and the Anti
Lincoln Tradition," available at www.historycooperative.org/journals/jala/24.1/
norman.html, accessed July 21, 2009.

Herbert K. Russell, *Edgar Lee Masters*, Urbana: University of Illinois Press, 2005.

## SOMERSET MAUGHAM

Hugh Leonard, "Cakes and Ale and a Dash of Vinegar," *Independent*, October 9, 1999, available at www.independent.ie/entertainment/news-gossip/cakes-and-ale-and-a-dash-of-vinegar-393194.html, accessed August 13, 2009.

Jeffrey Meyers, *Somerset Maugham: A Life*, New York: Knopf, 2004.

Ted Morgan, *Maugham: A Biography*, New York: Simon & Schuster, 1980.

D. G. Myers, "Posterity Makes Its Choice," A Commonplace Blog, April 13, 2009, available at http://dgmyers.blogspot.com/2009/04/posterity-makes-its-choice.html, accessed August 13, 2009.

Frank Wilson, "Author's Full Life Satisfies as Book," *Philadelphia Inquirer*, March 21, 2004.


## MARY MCCARTHY

Carol Brightman, *Writing Dangerously: Mary McCarthy and Her World*, New York: Clarkson Potter, 1992.

Frances Kiernan, *Seeing Mary Plain: A Life of Mary McCarthy*, New York: W.W. Norton & Company, 2002.


## H. L. MENCKEN

Arnold Leslie Lazarus, *The George Jean Nathan Reader*, Rutherford, NJ: Fairleigh Dickinson University Press, 1990.

"Gridiron Club," Wikipedia, available at http://en.wikipedia.org/wiki/Gridiron_Club, accessed August, 24, 2009.

Richard Lingeman, *Sinclair Lewis: Rebel from Main Street*, New York: Random House, 2002.

Mass Moments, "H. L. Mencken Arrested in Boston," available at http://massmoments.org/moment.cfm?mid=104, accessed August 20, 2009.

Terry Teachout, *The Skeptic: A Life of H. L. Mencken*, New York: HarperCollins, 2002.


## HENRY MILLER

Deirdre Bair, *Anaïs Nin: A Biography*, New York: Penguin, 1995.

Robert Ferguson, *Henry Miller: A Life*, New York: W.W. Norton & Company, 1991.

Suzanne Marrs, *Eudora Welty: A Biography*, Boston: Houghton Mifflin Harcourt, 2005.

Frances Wilson, *Literary Seductions*, London: Faber & Faber, 1999.


## JOHN MILTON

John Ashton, *Eighteenth Century Waifs*, Hurst & Blackett, 1887.

## YUKIO MISHIMA
Dennis Michael Annuzz, "November 25, 1970," available at http://dennismichaeliannuzz
.tripod.com/finalDay.html, accessed July 14, 2009.


## ANAÏS NIN
Deirdre Bair, *Anaïs Nin: A Biography*, New York: Penguin, 1995.


## EUGENE O'NEILL
Warren Hasting and Richard F. Weeks, "Episodes of Eugene O'Neill's Undergraduate
Days at Princeton," *Princeton University Library Chronicle* 29, no. 3 (spring 1968):
208–215.


## DOROTHY PARKER
Marion Meade, *Dorothy Parker: What Fresh Hell Is This?* New York: Penguin, 1989.


## BORIS PASTERNAK
Peter Finn, "A New Book Promises an Intriguing Twist to the Epic Tale," *Washington
Post*, January 29, 2007.
Mark Franchetti, "How the CIA Won Zhivago a Nobel," *Sunday Times*, January 14, 2007.


## SYLVIA PLATH
Sylvia Plath and Karen V. Kukil, *The Unabridged Journals of Sylvia Plath, 1950–1962*,
New York: Random House, 2000.
Obituary: Ted Hughes, *Daily Telegraph*, October 30, 1998, available at www
.telegraph.co.uk/news/obituaries/5886550/Ted-Hughes.html, accessed June 1,
2010.


## EDGAR ALLAN POE
Peter Ackroyd, *Poe: A Life Cut Short*, London: Chatto & Windus, 2008.
*Edgar Allan Poe: Poetry and Tales*, New York: The Library of America, 1984.
James M. Hutchisson, *Poe*, Jackson: University Press of Mississippi, 2005.
Kenneth Silverman, *Edgar A. Poe: Mournful and Never-Ending Remembrance*, New
York: Harper Perennial, 1992.


## ALEXANDER POPE
Helene Koon, *Colley Cibber*, Lexington: University Press of Kentucky, 1982.

## KATHERINE ANNE PORTER

Joan Givner, *Katherine Anne Porter: A Life*, New York: Simon & Schuster, 1982.


## EZRA POUND

Louis Menand, "The Pound Error," *New Yorker*, June 9, 2008.

Ira Bruce Nadel, *The Cambridge Companion to Ezra Pound*, Cambridge: Cambridge University Press, 2008.

"Social Credit," Wikipedia, available at http://en.wikipedia.org/wiki/Social_Credit, accessed July 9, 2009.


## MARCEL PROUST

William C. Carter, *Marcel Proust: A Life*, New Haven, CT: Yale University Press, 2002.

William C. Carter, *Proust in Love*, New Haven, CT: Yale University Press, 2006.


## ARTHUR RIMBAUD

Charles Nicholl, *Somebody Else: Arthur Rimbaud in Africa, 1880–91*, Chicago: University of Chicago Press, 1999.

Graham Robb, *Rimbaud: A Biography*, New York: W.W. Norton & Company, 2001.

Edmund White, "Teenage Dirtbag," *Guardian*, January 10, 2009, available at www .guardian.co.uk/books/2009/jan/10/arthur-rimbaud-edmund-white, accessed July 28, 2009.

"You Really Look Like a Dick!" available at www.nickelinthemachine.com/2007/12/ camden-town-verlaine-and-rimbaud-a-toilet-sid-sods-off-and-the-mcalpine -fusiliers, accessed July 28, 2009.


## THEODORE ROETHKE

Allan Seager, *The Glass House: The Life of Theodore Roethke*, Ann Arbor: University of Michigan Press, 1991.


## DANTE GABRIEL ROSSETTI

Nicholas A. Basbanes, *A Gentle Madness: Bibliophiles, Bibliomanes, and the Eternal Passion for Books*, New York: Henry Holt, 1995.

Walter Blumenthal, *Bookmen's Bedlam: An Olio of Literary Oddities*, New Brunswick, NJ: Rutgers University Press, 1955.


## JEAN-JACQUE ROUSSEAU

David Edmonds and John Eidinow, *Rousseau's Dog: Two Great Thinkers at War in the Age of Enlightenment*, New York: Ecco, 2006.

## VITA SACKVILLE-WEST

Nigel Nicolson, *Portrait of a Marriage: Vita Sackville-West and Harold Nicolson*, Chicago: University of Chicago Press, 1998.

Ann-Marie Priest, *Great Writers, Great Loves: The Reinvention of Love in the Twentieth Century*, Melbourne: Black, 2006.


## GEORGE SAND

Samuel Edwards, *George Sand*, New York: McKay, 1972.

Belinda Jack, *George Sand: A Woman's Life Writ Large*, New York: Knopf, 2000.

Joseph R. Orgel, *Undying Passion*, New York: William Morrow, 1985.


## WALTER SCOTT

David Hewitt, "Scott, Sir Walter (1771–1832)," *Oxford Dictionary of National Biography*, Oxford University Press, 2004, available at www.oxforddnb.com/view/article/24928, accessed October 24, 2004.


## CHARLES SEDLEY

John Scott, ed., *The London Magazine*, vol. 6, Taylor & Hessey, 1822.

Robert Lathan and William Matthews, eds., *The Diary of Samuel Pepys*, vol. 4, Berkeley and Los Angeles: University of California Press, 2000.


## ANNE SEXTON

Kelly Boler, *A Drinking Companion*, New York: Union Square Publishing, 2004.

Diane Wood Middlebrook, *Anne Sexton: A Biography*, Boston: Houghton Mifflin, 1991.


## WILLIAM SHAKESPEARE

James P. Bednarz, *Shakespeare and the Poets' War*, New York: Columbia University Press, 2001.

Robert Hendrickson, *American Literary Anecdotes*, New York: Facts on File, 1990.

Robert Hendrickson, *British Literary Anecdotes*, New York: Facts on File, 1990.

Daniel Henry Lambert, *Cartae Shakespeareanae*, London: George Bell & Sons, 1904.


## GEORGE BERNARD SHAW

Michael Holroyd, *Bernard Shaw, vol. 1: 1856–1898: The Search for Love*, London: Chatto & Windus, 1988.

## PERCY BYSSHE SHELLEY

Philip Gooden, *The Mammoth Book of Literary Anecdotes*, New York: Carroll & Graf, 2002.

John Gross, *The New Oxford Book of Literary Anecdotes*, New York: Oxford University Press, 2006.

Richard Holmes, *Shelley*, New York: New York Review of Books Classics, 2003.

Darby Lewes and Bob Stiklus, "Tan-yr-allt," available at www.rc.umd.edu/reference/misc/shelleysites/wales/tanyrallt/tanyrallt.html, accessed July 22, 2009.

Ann Wroe, *Being Shelley*, New York: Random House, 2008.


## RICHARD SHERIDAN

John Booth, *Creative Spirits*, London: André Deutsch, 1997.

Fintan O'Toole, *A Traitor's Kiss: A Life of Richard Sheridan*, New York: Farrar, Straus & Giroux, 1998.


## UPTON SINCLAIR

Anthony Arthur, *Radical Innocent: Upton Sinclair*, New York: Random House, 2006.

William Brevda, *Harry Kemp: The Last Bohemian*, Lewisburg, PA: Bucknell University Press, 1986.


## GEORGE O. SMITH

David Langford, "The Naughty Parts," available at www.ansible.co.uk/sfx/sfx054.html, accessed November 5, 2009.


## JOHN STEINBECK

Carlos Baker, *Ernest Hemingway: A Life Story*, New York: Scribner, 1969.

Jackson J. Benson, *The True Adventures of John Steinbeck, Writer*, New York: Viking, 1984.


## WALLACE STEVENS

Carlos Baker, *Ernest Hemingway: A Life Story*, New York: Scribner, 1969.

Jeffrey Meyers, *Hemingway: A Biography*, New York: Da Capo Press, 1999.


## JACQUELINE SUSANN

Michael Korda, *Another Life*, New York: Dell, 2000.

Barbara Seaman, *Lovely Me*, New York: Seven Stories Press, 1996.

## JONATHAN SWIFT

"The Predictions of Isaac Bickerstaff," available at www.museumofhoaxes.com/bickerstaff
.html, accessed August 2, 2003.

Jonathan Swift, "The Bickerstaff-Partridge Papers," available at http://etext.library
.adelaide.edu.au/s/s97b, accessed June 2, 2003.


## DYLAN THOMAS

Brendan Gill, *Here at the New Yorker*, New York: Random House, 1975.

Kathryn Hughes, "Drinking and Debauchery," *Independent*, May 18, 2008.

Kathryn Hughes, "Life with Dylan and Caitlin Thomas," *Daily Telegraph*, May 11, 2008.

Cahal Milmo, "Makers of Dylan Thomas Biopic Focus on Poet's Tangled Love Life," *Independent*, May 1, 2007.


## HENRY DAVID THOREAU

"'Burnt Woods': Ecological Insights into Thoreau's Unhappy Encounter with Forest Fire," *Thoreau Research Newsletter* 2, no. 3 (July 1991): 1–8.

Walter Harding, *The Days of Henry Thoreau*, Princeton: Princeton University Press, 1993.

Douglas T. Miller, *Henry David Thoreau: A Man for All Seasons*, Bridgewater, NJ: Replica Books, 2001.


## ALICE B. TOKLAS

Edward L. King, "Bernard Fay," available at www.masonicinfo.com/fay.htm, accessed July 10, 2009.

Janet Malcolm, *Two Lives: Gertrude and Alice*, New Haven, CT: Yale University Press, 2007.

James R. Mellow, *Charmed Circle: Gertrude Stein and Company*, New York: Henry Holt, 2003.


## LEO TOLSTOY

David Holbrook, *Tolstoy, Woman and Death: A Study of War and Peace and Anna Karenina*, Rutherford, NJ: Fairleigh Dickinson University Press, 1997.

A. N. Wilson, *Tolstoy*, New York: W.W. Norton & Company, 1988.


## MARK TWAIN

Alfred Paine, *Mark Twain's Notebook*, New York: Harper and Brothers, 1935.

Ron Powers, *Mark Twain: A Life*, New York: Free Press, 2005.

R. Kent Rasmussen, *Mark Twain A–Z*, New York: Oxford University Press, 1995.

Saki, "My Books Are Water; Those of the Great Geniuses Are Wine," available at http://my-nepenthe.blogspot.com/2004/03/my-books-are-water-those-of-great .html, accessed November 5, 2009.

Mark Twain and Michael Patrick Hearn, *The Annotated Huckleberry Finn*, New York: W.W. Norton & Company, 2001.

Mark Twain, Harriet Elinor Smith, and Edgar Marquess Branch, *Roughing It*, Berkeley and Los Angeles: University of California Press, 1993.


## PAUL VERLAINE

Edmund White, "Teenage Dirtbag," *Guardian*, January 10, 2009, available at www .guardian.co.uk/books/2009/jan/10/arthur-rimbaud-edmund-white, accessed July 28, 2009.

"You Really Look Like a Dick!" available at www.nickelinthemachine.com/2007/12/ camden-town-verlaine-and-rimbaud-a-toilet-sid-sods-off-and-the-mcalpine -fusiliers, accessed July 28, 2009.


## GORE VIDAL

Harry Kloman, "Political Animals: Vidal, Buckley and the '68 Conventions," available at www.pitt.edu/~kloman/debates.html, accessed September 3, 2009.

"On Mr. Buckley and Civility," *The Rush Limbaugh Show*, February 28, 2008, available at www.rushlimbaugh.com/home/daily/site_022808/content/01125106.guest.html, accessed July 10, 2009.

Gore Vidal, *Selected Essays of Gore Vidal*, New York: Vintage, 2008.


## VOLTAIRE

"Voltaire's Beatings: History House," available at www.historyhouse.com/in_history/ voltaire_rohan, accessed November 5, 2009.


## ELIZABETH VON ARNIM

Katie Roiphe, *Uncommon Arrangements*, New York: Random House, 2008.

H. G. Wells, *H. G. Wells in Love*, Boston: Little, Brown, 1984.


## HUGH WALPOLE

Hugh Leonard, "Cakes and Ale and a Dash of Vinegar," *Independent*, October 9, 1999, available at www.independent.ie/entertainment/news-gossip/cakes-and -ale-and-a-dash-of-vinegar-393194.html, accessed August 13, 2009.

Ted Morgan, *Maugham: A Biography*, New York: Simon & Schuster, 1980.

D. G. Myers, "Posterity Makes Its Choice," A Commonplace Blog, April 13, 2009, available at http://dgmyers.blogspot.com/2009/04/posterity-makes-its-choice.html, accessed August 13, 2009.

Jeffrey Myers, *Somerset Maugham: A Life*, New York: Knopf, 2004.


**H. G. WELLS**

H.C.G. Matthew, and Brian Harrison, *Dictionary of National Biography*, New York: Oxford University Press, 2004.

Katie Roiphe, *Uncommon Arrangements*, New York: Random House, 2008.

H. G. Wells, *H. G. Wells in Love*, Boston: Little, Brown, 1984.


**IDA B. WELLS**

Dennis Brindell Fradin and Judith Bloom Fradin, *Ida B. Wells: Mother of the Civil Rights Movement*, New York: Clarion Books, 2000.

"Ida B. Wells," Wikipedia, available at http://en.wikipedia.org/wiki/Ida_B._Wells, accessed November 4, 2009.


**EUDORA WELTY**

Robert Ferguson, *Henry Miller: A Life*, New York: W.W. Norton & Company, 1991.

Suzanne Marrs, *Eudora Welty: A Biography*, Boston: Houghton Mifflin Harcourt, 2005.


**REBECCA WEST**

Katie Roiphe, *Uncommon Arrangements*, New York: Random House, 2008.

H.C.G. Matthew, and Brian Harrison, *Dictionary of National Biography*, New York: Oxford University Press, 2004.


**EDITH WHARTON**

Hermione Lee, *Edith Wharton*, New York: Knopf, 2007.

R.W.B. Lewis, "Edith Wharton: The Beckoning Quarry," available at www.americanheritage.com/articles/magazine/ah/1975/6/1975_6_52.shtml, accessed September 10, 2009.

R.W.B. Lewis and Nancy Lewis, *The Letters of Edith Wharton*, New York: Scribner, 1988.

Marion Mainwaring, *Mysteries of Paris: The Quest for Morton Fullerton*, Hanover, NH: University Press of New England, 2001.


**E. B. WHITE**

Jill Lepore, "The Lion and the Mouse," *New Yorker*, July 21, 2008.

Julia Mucci, "Anne Carroll Moore: Our First Supervisor of Work with Children,"
    revised 2004, available at http://kids.nypl.org/parents/ocs_centennial_acm.cfm,
    accessed June 2, 2010.


## WALT WHITMAN
Justin Kaplan, *Walt Whitman: A Life*, New York: HarperCollins, 2003.


## OSCAR WILDE
Richard Ellmann, *Oscar Wilde*, London: Hamish Hamilton, 1987.
Neil McKenna, *The Secret Life of Oscar Wilde*, New York: Basic Books, 2005.
William Butler Yeats, *The Trembling of the Veil*, London: Werner Laurie, 1922.


## WILLIAM CARLOS WILLIAMS
William Carlos Williams, *The Autobiography of William Carlos Williams*, New York:
    New Directions, 1967.


## P. G. WODEHOUSE
David Langton, "Letter Reveals Wodehouse's Pain at Being Branded a Collaborator,"
    *Independent*, June 4, 2007, available at www.independent.co.uk/news/uk/this
    -britain/letter-reveals-wodehouses-pain-at-being-branded-a-collaborator-451677
    .html, accessed September 1, 2009.
John Simpson, "Why A. A. Had It in for P. G.," *Daily Telegraph*, August 31, 1996.
Iain Sproat, *Wodehouse at War*, London: Ticknor & Fields, 1981.


## VIRGINIA WOOLF
Quentin Bell, *Virginia Woolf: A Biography*, Boston: Houghton Mifflin, 1974.
"Dreadnought Hoax," Wikipedia, available at http://en.wikipedia.org/wiki/Dreadnought_
    Hoax, accessed September 17, 2009.
Phyllis Rose, *Woman of Letters: A Life of Virginia Woolf*, London: Routledge, 1986.


## WILLIAM WORDSWORTH
R. Shelton Mackenzie, *Life of Charles Dickens*, Peterson & Brothers, 1870.


## RICHARD WRIGHT
Michel Fabre, *The Unfinished Quest of Richard Wright*, Urbana: University of Illinois
    Press, 1993.

Debbie Levy, *Richard Wright: A Biography*, Minneapolis: Twenty-First Century Books, 2007.

## EXTRA RESOURCES

Kelly Boler, *A Drinking Companion*, New York: Union Square Publishing, 2004.

Christopher Cerf and Victor S. Navasky, *The Experts Speak*, New York: Pantheon, 1984.

Edmond de Goncourt and Jules de Goncourt, *Pages from the Goncourt Journals*, New York: New York Review of Books, 2006.

Clifton Fadiman and André Bernard, *Bartlett's Book of Anecdotes*, New York: Little, Brown and Company, 2000.

Mark Harris, "Checkout Time at the Asylum," *New York*, November 16, 2008, available at http://nymag.com/news/features/52176, accessed December 11, 2008.

Robert Hendrickson, *British Literary Anecdotes*, New York: Facts on File, 1990.

Peter Kemp, *The Oxford Dictionary of Literary Quotations*, New York: Oxford University Press, 2003.

David Lehman, *The Oxford Book of American Poetry*, New York: Oxford University Press, 2006.

Randy F. Nelson, *The Almanac of American Letters*, New York: William Kaufmann Inc., 1981.

Joseph Randolph Orgel, *Undying Passion*, New York: William Morrow, 1985.

# Index